ROMSEY ABBEY THROUGH THE CENTURIES

by

JUDY WALKER

PENDRAGON PRESS
PENNINGTON

A PENDRAGON PRESS Book

Copyright © 1993 Judy Walker

First published in Great Britain in 1993 by
Pendragon Press Pennington

All rights reserved

British Library Cataloguing-in-Publication Data
A catalogue record for this book is available from
the British Library

This book was designed and typeset by
Pendragon Press Pennington
38 South Street, Lymington, SO41 8DX

Printed by J W Arrowsmith Ltd, Bristol and London

In memory of
Michael
who loved the Abbey
and started the ball rolling

FOREWORD FROM THE VICAR

I am grateful to Judy Walker for this book, which makes readily accessible a wide range of historical information about Romsey Abbey, one of the great buildings of the world

The book will be of interest on two fronts. On the one hand this ancient building is the centre of a lively church life in a busy parish. It is natural that today's worshippers should be interested in the building they use and in those who have used it in former generations and centuries.

On the other hand there are those who journey from near and far to visit the church. This more substantial book increases, in a highly readable account, the range of information offered in Judy Walker's earlier publication *The Illustrated Guide to Romsey Abbey*. Many visitors and pilgrims will be glad to read what she has to offer.

I offer my gratitude and congratulations to her for her work, particularly bearing in mind that profits from the sale of the book will help towards the restoration of the Abbey Organ, and also urgent work on the bell frame, bells and tower. I trust that others will have as much pleasure as I have had in reading it.

Neil Crawford-Jones

PREFACE AND ACKNOWLEDGEMENTS

The purpose of this book is two-fold. In the main text, I aim to provide a historical record of the abbey church, both through the centuries during which it belonged to a famous Benedictine nunnery and in its subsequent role as a great parish church. Secondly, in the series of appendices I supply more detailed information and place on record the results of some efforts at historical research in the hope of making a small contribution to the corpus which already exists.

In any undertaking of this kind one is heavily dependent both on work already published and on knowledge amassed by others and I am deeply grateful to all who have assisted me and provided constructive advice and corrections, particularly to Frank Green and Ian Scott of TVAT and to the committee of the LTVAS Group who have all given most generously of their time and expertise. I also wish to thank Diana Coldicott who has answered all my queries most patiently and promptly. Many others have provided invaluable help, including Diane Hargreaves who cares for the abbey fabric, Tresta Grimwood who shared her knowledge of Romanesque architecture, Betty Munday of Cambridge who vetted my Latin translations and Barbara Dancy who has lent me her antiquarian books on Romsey. I have received specialist advice from Dr John Harvey (on medieval masons), Michael Archer of the V & A Museum, Kensington (on medieval glass) and Professor A G Watson (on the psalter) and benefited greatly from the information shared with me by Anna Hulbert while engaged on conservation work in the abbey, by Simon Owers while he was studying the capitals for a dissertation, and by Christopher Collier in discussions on his Anglo-Saxon studies. There are others, too many to name, who have provided interesting items of information and I record my gratitude to them all.

I also thank all those who have supplied me with pictures or have waived copyright. Acknowledgements will be found in the List of Illustrations, but I particularly wish to thank Stanley Sales and C T Drew who have allowed me to use their excellent photographs.

My final expression of gratitude must be to Gillian Morgan of Pendragon Press who has guided me through the intricacies of modern technology to produce this book and has taken no personal profit from the enterprise.

While endeavouring to correct some of the erroneous statements which appeared in older guidebooks, I shall undoubtedly have committed some blunders of my own, and for these I am solely responsible. While I have collected under one cover much information which was previously unrecorded, I am aware that because of limitations of space this account of the abbey church is still far from comprehensive. I offer it as a basis for the next generation of abbey historians.

Judy Walker
Romsey
January 1993

ABBREVIATIONS

BL	British Library
HFC	Proceedings of the Hampshire Field Club
LTVAS	Lower Test Valley Archaeological Study Group
P & P	Pots and Papers (LTVAS occasional Journal)
TVAT	Test Valley Archaeological Trust
V & A	Victoria and Albert Museum, London

TABLE OF CONTENTS

Page No.

1.	Saxon Times	1
2.	The Building of the Norman Church	13
3.	Pre-Reformation Paintings in the Church	32
4.	Pre-Reformation Monuments, Carvings and Relics	41
5.	Life in the Medieval Abbey	49
6.	The Church and the Nunnery	62
7.	The Church: Interior Changes	69
8.	Post-Reformation Monuments and Memorials	85
9.	'Make a joyful noise to God'	97
	1. Romsey Organs	97
	2. Summoned by Bells	106
10.	Stained Glass Windows	112
11.	Glimpses and Portraits	120
12.	The Little Town with the Large Church	139
Appendix 1	Abbesses of Romsey	i
Appendix 2	Vicars of Romsey	iv
Appendix 3	A Re-assessment of King Edgar's Charter for Romsey	vii
Appendix 4	The Two Historiated Capitals	xii

Appendix 5   Dates and Charters relating to the move of Mary de Blois from Lillechurch and her election as Abbess of Romsey   xvii

Appendix 6   The Provenance of the Fifteenth Century Psalter   xix

Appendix 7   Explanation of alternative years of death found on tombstones   xx

Appendix 8   John Kent Memorial   xxi

Appendix 9   The Organ Appeal   xxii

Appendix 10   Twentieth Century Gifts and Acquisitions   xxv

Examples of architectural styles to be found in the Abbey   xxvi

Bibliography   xxvii

Plan of Romsey Abbey   xxx

List of Illustrations   xxxi

CHAPTER ONE

SAXON TIMES

First impressions on entering Romsey Abbey are of a magnificent church built in the Norman style. The visitor has to look more closely to find evidence that it was once the church of a famous Benedictine convent. An even more diligent search will reveal hints and traces of the nunnery's Saxon past.

The most obvious of these traces are the two famous Saxon roods and the foundations of an earlier church visible in the north transept. There is also a relic from a Saxon grave and a reminder in the very name of St.Ethelfleda who is coupled with the Virgin Mary as patron of the church. These all take us back to the abbey's pre-Conquest history.

The Foundation of the Saxon Nunnery

The commonly accepted foundation of the abbey by Edward the Elder, the son of Alfred the Great, at the beginning of the 10th century (907 AD is the date usually quoted) is based on statements from chroniclers writing in the 12th century or later, whose knowledge was not first-hand.

Florence of Worcester, who died in 1118, records that in the year 967 King Edgar the Peaceful placed nuns in the monastery at Romsey, which his grandfather, Edward the Elder, had built.[1] (The term 'monastery' originally applied to houses of either monks or nuns.) Peter de Langtoft, in the following century, also gives Edward the Elder as founder and says that two of his daughters were nuns:

Elfleda and Saynt Eadburgh that lyved holy life.[2]

The 14th century *Liber de Hyda*, from the abbey at Winchester which had fraternal ties with Romsey, refers to:

Elfleda, holy and dedicated to God, who lies at Romsey.[3]

The tradition that Edward the Elder placed nuns at Romsey and that his daughter Elfleda took the veil here is probably correct. Whether a religious house had existed in Romsey before that date is a question to which no complete answer can be given, but clues have been emerging from archaeological and other studies which, seen in the light of the history of Christianity in Wessex before the 10th century, have been pointing to an earlier foundation on the site than had previously been guessed at.

Early Monasticism in Wessex

The spread of Christianity among the West Saxons, after the conversion and baptism of their king, Cynegils, in 635 AD, did not proceed at a steady pace. There were lapses into paganism as chieftain warred against chieftain, and in 793 AD there began the Viking attacks against this island which continued sporadically over the next two centuries.

During peaceful interludes monasteries were founded, only to be swept away again by another invasion. Alfred the Great (r.871-899 AD) championed the Church, founded monasteries and encouraged education for both sexes. His son, Edward the Elder, continued the revival, but further Viking attacks and the troubled times resulted in the monasteries practically disappearing within little more than a generation. Eadwig (r.955-959 AD) was positively hostile to the Church. Fortunately, his reign was brief and his brother Edgar, who succeeded him, was a man of faith and a keen Church supporter. He was shocked by the state in which he found the religious houses and is quoted by the chronicler, William of Malmesbury, as saying:

> *All the monasteries in my realm, to the outward sight, are nothing but worm-eaten and rotten lumber and boards; and what is worse, they are almost empty and devoid of divine service.*[4]

Edgar is said to have rebuilt and re-endowed no fewer than 40 monasteries. His re-founding of Romsey Abbey is well recorded. A re-assessment of the authenticity of his charter for Romsey and a translation of the Latin text will be found in Appendix Three. The shadowy past of the abbey before the 10th century has to be seen against the background of the ebb and flow of the Christian faith in general and the monastic life in particular during the middle Saxon period, although there is no evidence in the southern Test Valley area of a complete relapse into paganism.

2

Possible Romsey-Nursling links before 900 AD

In the early centuries after the conversion, before the development of the parochial system, the country was divided into a few huge dioceses. To carry on the work of mission, the bishops planted groups of priests in the more important centres which became known as 'minsters'.

Collier[5] applies the term 'minster' to the concept of a community of men and women flourishing between Nursling and Romsey — two settlements close to each other on the River Test — and acting as a centre for prayer, learning and mission in the 8th and 9th centuries. Collier calls attention to the teaching given by Winfrith, later known as St.Boniface, at a site close to Romsey usually identified with Nursling. This centre must have existed in the 8th century but no traces of an abbey have been found at Nursling. The writer suggests that monastery and nunnery originally formed part of one large minster and that the nuns' convent evolved from this.

Evidence for an early foundation date in Romsey

The evidence is circumstantial and may be categorized as archaeological, geographical and historical.

Archaeological: It was assumed until relatively recently that Romsey was a 'green field' site until the abbey was founded by Edward the Elder and that the town then grew up around it to serve its needs. However, excavations by the Test Valley Archaeological Trust have revealed an iron-smelting site close to the abbey in the Middle to Late Saxon period. Other excavations in and around the church have brought to light signs of rammed chalk footings of a stone church pre-dating the one already uncovered (*See section below on Saxon foundations in the north transept*), while the discovery of some early charcoal-packed burials on a different alignment has pointed to the existence of an even earlier stone church on the site.

Geographical: It has been pointed out that Romsey held a strategic position on the routes between Southampton, Winchester and the west country. With its convenient position as a gravel 'island' on the Test, it was a likely site for early settlement and the planting of a 'minster'.

3

Historical: Another hint to an early date for the foundation of the abbey is that it possessed a relic of St. Bathild, a Saxon lady who married King Clovis II and was the mother of three Frankish kings. She was patron saint of the abbey of Chelles where her remains were translated in 833 AD. In 855 AD Alfred's father, King Ethelwulf, married, as his second wife, Judith, the daughter of Charles the Bold. Judith's mother was protectress of the abbey of Chelles and might well have given a relic of this Saxon saint to her daughter to bestow on an English nunnery.

The Saxon Abbey from 907 AD

We may return now to what is known of the Saxon abbey in the period between 907 AD and the building of the Romanesque church begun about 1120 AD. Whether or not Edward the Elder was the first founder of a nunnery in Romsey, there is no reason to doubt that he was a benefactor and that he placed his daughter Elfleda here, probably as abbess. She is sometimes called Ethelfleda in documents, but she is referred to in this book as Elfleda to avoid confusion with the later Ethelfleda, patron saint of the abbey, whose story is recounted below.

In the time of King Edgar, under the influence of Bishop Ethelwold, a council of Church leaders held at Winchester had agreed on a reform of all monastic houses in England so that they would observe a common rule based on the Rule of St. Benedict. This agreement, known as the *Regularis Concordia* was applied to Romsey Abbey and, along with religious reform, Edgar seems to have been responsible for a considerable extension of the buildings. The new buildings are said to have been completed in 974 AD and dedicated by Bishop Ethelwold in the presence of the king and his nobles on Christmas Day.

Peter de Langtoft praises Edgar's pious work in these words:

> *Mikille he wirshipped God, and served our Lady;*
> *The Abbey of Rumege he feffed richely*
> *With rentes full gode and kirkes of pris,*
> *He did ther in of Nunnes a hundreth ladies.*[6]

The number of nuns in King Edgar's time may be exaggerated, but the figure was reached in the abbey's heyday several centuries later. By 1300

4

the bishop issued a rebuke to the convent for admitting an excessive number. Presumably there were then over a hundred as thirty years later we find the numbers reduced to ninety-one.

As abbess of the enlarged and reformed nunnery, Edgar appointed Merwenna (many variations are given of her name) but nothing is known to us about this lady. The king evidently held her in very high esteem for when his eldest son Edmund died in childhood, he chose Romsey Abbey to be the little boy's last resting-place. Merwenna's signature is prominent among witnesses to two charters from King Edgar to Croyland Abbey near Peterborough. Doubts have been raised about the authenticity of these charters, but, even if forged, they are evidence that the abbess was recognized as a person of consequence whose signature carried weight. Merwenna was later canonized but her reputation became overshadowed by her more famous protégée, Ethelfleda.

St. Ethelfleda

According to the most reliable accounts, Ethelfleda was the daughter of one of Edgar's nobles called Ethelwold. When he died, Edgar married his widow Elfrida who was Ethelfleda's stepmother. The king placed the orphaned girl in the care of the saintly Abbess Merwenna at Romsey, where she later took the veil.

In a 14th century document, *Lives of English Saints* [7], the love between the abbess and the young girl is movingly recounted:

Seal of St. Ethelfleda

> And right well did the Abbess Merwenna behave as a sweet mother to Ethelfleda and Ethelfleda as a loving daughter to Merwenna.

The book describes Ethelfleda's holy life. As a self-imposed penance she used to slip outside at night, undress and stand naked in a running stream

5

(presumably a branch of the Test), where she poured forth prayers to God. The queen, staying at the abbey on one occasion, became suspicious and followed her. When she saw the young girl's devotion, she was so overcome that she fell to the ground in a faint.

A number of stories are related of miracles which Ethelfleda performed: for example, when darkness fell, she was able to read the Scriptures by light which glowed from her fingertips; as abbess, she once gave away all the abbey money to the destitute, but after she had prayed the coffers were miraculously refilled.

These stories were told to illustrate Ethelfleda's character, which is described as:

> *abundant in virtues, generous in alms, constant in watches, in speech vigilant, in mind humble, of joyful countenance and kindly mannered to the poor.*

One could wish that the writer had more historical information to give us about Ethelfleda, as she lived through stirring times. She apparently fled to Winchester with the other nuns when the abbey was raided by the Danes; was elected abbess after their return; and may have been responsible for the rebuilding or repair of the Saxon church whose foundations may be seen in the north transept.

After Merwenna's death, the next abbess was Elwina (see below), presumably because Ethelfleda was still too young, but on Elwina's death she was succeeded by Ethelfleda who continued to be an example of humility and saintliness. She died on October 23rd in a year around 1016 and in due course she was canonized. Later her name was coupled with St.Mary the Virgin in the dedication of the Norman abbey church.

Abbess Elwina

Elwina was abbess for a brief but dramatic period in the abbey's history between Merwenna's and Ethelfleda's periods of office around the time of the millenium. The sporadic Viking attacks of the preceding centuries, mainly directed at plunder, had given way to larger-scale, organized invasions directed at conquest. These took place during the reign of the incompetent Ethelred, in the years between 988 and 1016. Expeditions from Denmark were led by their king, Swein Forkbeard, and his son Cnut, who eventually took the throne after Ethelred's death.

During one of these invasions, Swein advanced into Wessex, ravaging the countryside. The legend is that Elwina, the newly-elected abbess, was praying at mass before the high altar when she saw a vision of the Danes attacking the abbey and burning the church. The nuns hastily packed their treasures and took refuge in the convent known as Nunnaminster in Winchester where they were safe within the walls of the fortified city. It used to be thought that the series of medallions painted on a wall of the ambulatory recount this story, although later expert opinion has suggested that they are part of a life of St.Nicholas (see below p.32).

Foundations of the Saxon church in the North Transept

The nuns returned to Romsey a few years later when peace was restored. It is not certain whether the abbey church had been destroyed or only damaged during the Danish raid. It is likely that the stone church (whose foundations were only discovered in 1900 during renewal of the flooring) was the one which was repaired and possibly extended at this time. This was certainly the church which was standing a hundred years later when the building of a larger Norman-style church was begun. The curve of the eastern apse of the Saxon church reaches approximately to the present chancel step, so it was perfectly possible to leave that church intact for worship while the choir and east ends of the transepts of the new church were being built. At that stage a temporary screen seems to have been erected across the completed section so that it could be used for services while the old Saxon church was demolished and the new nave built on its site.

Plaited hair found in a lead coffin [8]

Mention has already been made of the discovery by archaeologists of some early Saxon charcoal burials. Excavations made during the course of repairs to the church normally have to be minutely recorded but then filled up again. However, one

7

somewhat gruesome but interesting relic from an early burial remains visible. It came to light in 1839 when workmen were digging a grave in the church. In a lead coffin lined with oak a head of hair was found resting on a wooden pillow. According to the sexton, nothing else remained in the coffin except one finger bone which fell to dust on contact with the air. The coffin was discovered four or five feet below floor level in the easternmost bay of the south aisle, next to the south transept. It was about five feet long and wider at the head than the foot. It was made from three pieces of sheet lead which were overlapped and welded together without soldering. The burial seems to pre-date the foundations of the late Saxon church because it lay on a different alignment. It must have been the grave of wealthy or royal person to have been placed in such a coffin in such a position. Experts believe that it is Middle to Late Saxon in date. Unfortunately the coffin has been lost to the church and we only have contemporary descriptions, but the hair is kept, along with a few other items of historical interest, in a display case in the north-west corner of the church.

The two Saxon Roods

These two carved stone crucifixes were transferred by the nuns to the present church when the old Saxon church was demolished. Their exact date is uncertain, but experts suggest the last quarter of the 10th century for the small rood and the early years of the 11th century for the larger one.

The small rood (see front cover illustration) is now behind the altar in St.Anne's chapel where it is framed by part of a 15th century oak parclose screen. (In the course of its history, the rood seems to have stood in different parts of the church, may have been hidden for some centuries to avoid mutilation, and at one time may even, as appears from an old illustration, have been placed outside under the west gable.)

Although small, the rood shows a wealth of detail with figures and foliage in low relief. Christ on the cross is flanked by Our Lady and St.John. On the arms of the cross two angels with wands wait to escort the Saviour into heaven. At its foot are two Roman soldiers, one thrusting a lance into His side and the other offering a sponge of vinegar. The overall impression is not a scene of death but of victory: Christ reigns from a tree which is sprouting with new life.

A similar composition is said to be found on the Alnmouth Cross in Northumberland, both depending on the same imported models and both deriving from Carolingian iconography.

Even in the 18th century there were traces to show that the Romsey rood had once been ornate with gold and jewels. This fact and its probable date suggest that it was a royal gift. Possible donors are King Edgar or King Cnut. Cnut, in spite of his youthful pillaging of monasteries, entirely changed character after he became king, supported the Church and was a generous benefactor of abbeys. In the *Liber Vitae* of Hyde there is a picture of him and Queen Emma presenting a large gold cross to the New Minster. He might well have given a a similar gift to Romsey.

The large rood, which is almost life-size, shows Christ on a plain Latin cross with the Hand of God pointing down to him from heaven. It is sculptured in high relief on three stones, the body occupying one of them with the arms on the other two. It is on the west-facing outer wall of the south transept where, until the Dissolution, it would have been protected from the weather by the cloisters and passed daily by the nuns as they made their way in procession into the church for services. An oil lamp was probably kept burning in a recess in the wall to the right of the rood.

Angle of the south transept, Saxon rood and Norman doorway before restoration

9

There are signs that the rood was moved to this spot after the transept wall was completed: thin stones above the arms of the cross appear to have been put in after the crucifix was inserted to fill a gap left by the removal of the original stones.

The rood was probably an integral part of the earlier Saxon church (above the chancel arch or over the west door) and so could only be moved when the eastern part of the Norman church was usable for worship and the earlier church could be demolished (see Chapter Two). It may have been part of a larger composition, flanked by the figures of St.Mary and St.John.

In 1977 the ground beneath the rood was lowered to its original level and a stone pavement laid in order to protect it from damage by damp. It still remains vulnerable to the elements.

This sculpture, like the smaller one, is said to derive ultimately from Carolingian court art. The treatment of the body shows naturalism, but in the Byzantine tradition it shows Christ reigning and serene under the approving hand of the Father. In spite of defacement through weathering, it is apparent that the eyes are open and the face youthful with a short, curly beard. The body is draped from waist to knee and the legs are uncrossed and rest on a small plinth. The typical figure of Christ with legs crossed and feet fastened to the cross by a single nail, with which we are more familiar, was not adopted until the 13th century.

The 'Hand of God' is seen on coins of Ethelred's reign which were stamped at Winchester in 996 AD. Examples of it are also to be found in a drawing of a crucifix in the MS of Archbishop Ælfric's sermons dated 994, now in the British Museum, and in other southern England MSS of the 10th and 11th centuries. This hand used to be visible in two other Hampshire churches, Breamore and Headbourne Worthy. In both these churches the figures were savagely mutilated in the 16th century and only their outlines remain. At Breamore, unlike Romsey, Christ's head is bent by suffering, indicating a somewhat later date. The hand of God now appears just as a bulge but projects downwards from wavy lines representing cloud or sky. At Headbourne Worthy the rood was carved in stone on what was originally the outer west wall of the church above a Saxon doorway. Christ is flanked by Our Lady and St.John and one can see where the hand of God appears from a cloud but only shadowy outlines of the figures are left.

SOURCES

TVAT (A fuller account of the archaeology will be found in the forth-coming monograph *Excavation at Romsey Abbey* 1973-1991 by I.Scott *et al.* to be published by HFC, sponsored by English Heritage).

Coldicott, *Hampshire Nunneries*

Collier, *Romsey Minster in SaxonTimes*, HFC vol.46

Hunter Blair, *Anglo-Saxon England*

Moorman, *A History of the Church in England*

Coatsworth, 'Late pre-Conquest Sculptures' in *Bishop Æthelwold* ed. B.Yorke

REFERENCES

1.   Chronicle, p.103
2.   Langtoft transl. by Robert of Brunne quoted F.G.Walker, *Short History of Romsey*, p.17
3.   Ed.Birch, *Liber de Hyda* p.112
4.   Quoted C.Spence, *Handbook* 2nd ed. p.7
5.   Collier, *op.cit.* p.44
6.   Walker, *op.cit.* p.17
7.   Quoted Liveing, pp.19-26
8.   *Gentleman's Magazine*, August 1840

Romsey Abbey 1895

CHAPTER TWO

THE BUILDING OF THE NORMAN CHURCH

(AUTHOR'S NOTE: The architectural complexities of the building are outside the scope of this chapter which covers only a broad outline of the building stages, the use to which the different parts of the church were put and those details which are often the subject of visitors' comments and queries.[1])

Historical Background

The figure who forms a link between the Saxon and Norman history of the church is Eadyth, known after her marriage to King Henry I as Matilda. She was the elder daughter of Queen Margaret of Scotland and, with her sister Mary, was educated in the abbey in the care her aunt, Margaret's sister Christina, who was a nun. Her story has been told many times: some of the details are disputable but the broad outlines are well attested.

Margaret, Christina and their young brother, Edgar Atheling, were grandchildren of Edmund Ironside, a direct descendant of the Saxon royal line. They had been brought up in exile in Hungary but returned to England and were entertained first at the court of Edward the Confessor. Later, they were given hospitality in Scotland by the king, Malcolm III, who courted and married Margaret. It is this king, known as Malcolm Canmore (the Great Head) who is acclaimed the rightful king after the usurper Macbeth was slain in Shakespeare's drama of that name. This Celtic king and famous warrior was killed near Alnwick in 1093 while fighting against William Rufus. Margaret, who was already ill, followed him quickly to the grave. Her zealous faith and high principles are revealed in her letters to Archbishop Lanfranc, her spiritual father, and she was canonized by Pope Innocent IV in 1250.

It is not surprising that the young Eadyth-Matilda, daughter of this union, was a girl of spirit who only achieved her reputation for piety later, after she became queen. According to the story, William Rufus, who saw that marriage to a descendant of King Alfred would be popular among his Saxon subjects, came into the abbey on the pretext of seeing the rose garden but really to take a look at the young princess. Christina, knowing his dissolute reputation, had taken the precaution of making her niece wear a veil. William — never an enthusiast for marriage — was persuaded that the girl had already taken religious vows and abandoned the project. Some time later he was shot by an arrow while hunting in the New Forest and his body (so the story goes) was conveyed to Winchester through Romsey on a cart belonging to a charcoal-burner called Purkiss. His brother Henry then seized the throne and soon proposed marriage in his turn. Henry was more acceptable as a prospective husband and Eadyth was willing, but objections were raised that she was already a nun under vows and not free to marry.

Her spirited denial to Archbishop Anselm, written in Latin, that she had ever taken vows or willingly worn the veil is evidence on the one hand of her strong character and on the other of a sound education which enabled her to conduct a correspondence in Latin. Anselm was persuaded by her arguments and himself performed the wedding ceremony. Christina moved at some point to Wilton Abbey, presumably accompanied by her nieces, so Wilton rather than Romsey may have been the setting for part of this story.[2]

After her marriage, Matilda became a very active consort to Henry and was engaged in numerous good works which earned her the title of 'Good Queen Maud'. Even though Henry, in the manner of monarchs of his time, was a far from faithful husband, her death in 1118, followed only two years later by the drowning of his only son in the White Ship, left the king heart-broken. This brings us to the year 1120, the year when the building of Romsey's great new church is believed to have begun. No other name of a great patron is known. Did Henry make a substantial contribution as a memorial to his wife who had been brought up in the abbey? The suggestion has been made,[3] but positive proof is lacking.

William II had been a rapacious king who seized Church revenues for his own use and had little time for religion. He had allowed Church reforms begun by the Conqueror to lapse, but under Henry there began a period of orderly administration which became a golden age for Anglo-Norman monasticism. There was an influx of wealth and an enormous impulse for founding and extending monasteries. Churches throughout the country were being rebuilt in the romanesque style which was first introduced by Edward the Confessor who had spent his youth in Normandy. Their massive piers, thick walls and round-headed windows had all the solidity and strength of Norman castles. Romsey Abbey, with its royal connections and nuns drawn from the noblest

Anglo-Norman families, would have attracted a great deal of wealth quite apart from any money that the king himself may have given. It evidently decided that it could afford to follow the fashion of the day and build a larger and more magnificent church in the new Norman style.

The Planning of the Building

There were fairly straightforward geometric principles known to masons of the time, which were based on groups of squares.[4] At Romsey the plan is cruciform and the width of the church at the transepts is approximately half its total length. The original architect or master mason would have planned the overall size and proportions of the church and made drawings to scale as well as marking out the ground plan. Building then took place in stages and it was well over a century before the final phase was completed. In the course of that time changes in style were introduced and minor details were altered, but the church retained its overall character of simplicity and unity.

The nuns naturally wanted the new church to stand on the same site as the existing Saxon one, that is to say, on the northern side of the convent buildings — the usual site for a monastic church where the massive walls would help to provide the domestic buildings with some protection from bad weather.

Chapter One described how the new building was begun some distance to the east of the older church which meant that the nuns could continue to hold their services for some years in the Saxon building until the new chancel, choir aisles and most of the transepts were completed. Their worship during this period would have been disturbed only by the inevitable noise and dust. A temporary wall across the new chancel may have provided a makeshift church while the Saxon building was being demolished, or it may have been possible to retain the Saxon nave for worship for a considerable time. Problems must have arisen at the point where the southern transept wall of the Saxon church crossed the building line of the new nave and may have abutted on a cloister and domestic range of buildings. These would have had to be overcome before the building of the new nave could continue.

The East End

The plan at Romsey followed the general English preference in the twelfth century for a square east end. Although this was broken by a small twin-celled

15

chapel extending eastwards (later replaced by a larger one with east windows in the Decorated style), the two small apsed chapels at the north and south corners of the east end do not project, but are built into the thickness of the wall which is straight on the outside.

The passage which runs behind the high altar and joins these two eastern apses is commonly known as the retro-choir or ambulatory. Here and in the two choir aisles the pillars are surmounted by interesting carved capitals.

The Carved Capitals

There are some 36 sculptures on the capitals. Very little attention has been paid to them because they are tucked away at the far end of the church and many are difficult to see, even though there is more artificial and natural light available today than there was in Norman times.

It is possible to find some logic in the way the carvings are sited, although the picture is incomplete as we cannot tell what decoration there was within the demolished Lady chapel. The capitals facing inwards into the choir are left plain, presumably because the nuns came there for divine service and were expected to be concentrating on their prayers and not looking around. The bulk of the carvings lie on what would have been a processional route from the choir, through to the north choir aisle, round the retro-choir, past the eastern chapel, down the south choir aisle and out into the cloisters where the clergy would bless the convent buildings before the procession returned to the church through the south entrance.

There was a great love for processions in the medieval Church and this was the kind of route which would have been taken every Sunday. As the procession moved slowly and the clergy stopped for prayers at all the altars, there was plenty of time to look around, to be enlightened or entertained or reminded of the past.

The craftsmen who specialized in decorative sculptures probably followed drawings in a workbook and had considerable freedom in their choice of subject. A number of different hands seem to have been at work, representing a variety of styles and influences. One frequently repeated design shows a fanciful mask decorated with scrolls. In the retro-choir, there are beasts with human faces and two scenes from 'The Labours of the Month', showing a man reaping corn (September) and warming his hands by the fire (February). These were probably copied originally from illuminated manuscripts.

At the southern end of the retrochoir are stylized leaf designs. These, together with smiling lions and masks with scrolls, are all to be found in the crypt of Canterbury cathedral, where the quality is superior.

Stylized leaves

Lively scenes in scallops

Next, there are a number of capitals with scallops which usually hold some kind of fantastic bird or beast. Finally, there are two so-called 'historiated' capitals on the easternmost pillars of the north and south choir aisles, facing outwards. They evidently tell a story but their interpretation is obscure and has generated more heat than light in the past. The arguments are discussed in Appendix Four.

Historiated capital in north choir aisle

Historiated capital from south choir aisle

The Chancel

The Norman work is seen at its best in the chancel. The austerity of the great, rounded arches between the massive clustered piers is relieved by zigzag moulding round the arches and a frieze of billet pattern which runs right round between the main arcading and the gallery. The pillars enclose three bays each side of the chancel. Two further archways behind the altar would have taken the eyes of worshippers through to the eastern chapel with its twin altars. They may have contained the relics of the abbey's two saints, Merwenna and Ethelfleda.

There is an unusual feature in the gallery: within each main arch there are two sub-arches and the open space above them is divided by a colonnette. This small column is a curiosity: architecturally it performs no useful function as there can be no downward thrust from the centre of an arch. Further down the nave the feature is abandoned, as though it was realized that its pointless insertion was unpleasing. It is unique in this country, but curiously at Southwell Minster small stumps may be seen projecting downwards from the centre of each main arch of the gallery, as though a similar column was intended but then abandoned.

The Tower Crossing

As originally designed, the tower above the crossing was open to its roof. It was not until the seventeenth century that the bells were housed on the roof and a ceiling in fine Jacobean style placed above the crossing in order to create the ringing chamber above. The full story of the bells will be found in Chapter Nine.

NE view of chancel c.1826

Norman arcading round the tower crossing

INTERIOR of
SOUTH
TRANSEPT

21

In 1847 the ringing chamber was altered and the floor was raised about 12 feet to reveal from ground level the handsome Norman arcading round the crossing which previously had been blocked from view.

The Transepts

The north and south transepts both have eastern apses, originally chapels, but now separated off as vestries. They differ considerably from each other in their decoration and both their west windows have undergone alteration, although for different reasons. In the north transept, the reason for piercing through the west wall and later closing it again with the present west window will become apparent later in the chapter, in the section headed The Parish Church.

The west wall and windows of the south transept have occasioned much speculation. There are several points to be noted:

1. There is a straight join between this wall and the nave aisle wall, showing that there was a break in construction.

2. Delay in completing the west wall was probably caused by an upper storey of the existing convent buildings which was in the way.

3. The outer arches of the triplet windows were originally left blank and not glazed, presumably for a similar reason.

4. This would be the obvious site for a night stair by which the nuns could enter the church from their dormitory for the night office without having to go outside. This was its usual position in Benedictine Houses.

5. In the course of restoration there has been considerable alteration to the triplet windows, as may most clearly be seen from the outside.

The Nave

On each side at the top of the nave there is a giant cylindrical column which stretches up into the gallery. These two pillars were probably built at the same time as the crossing tower to ensure its safety and may have marked the first major pause in the building programme. Such a giant column gives a great feeling of height, but with only one capital from which arches can spring the

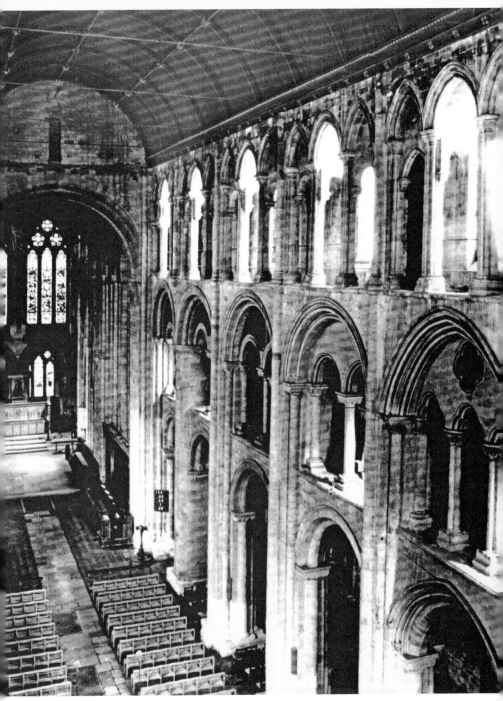

South side of the nave

conjunction with the lower arcade is slightly awkward. A similar arrangement is to be found in Oxford Cathedral and in the choir of Jedburgh Abbey. The latter site is interesting because Jedburgh, although so far away, may have been influenced by Romsey. It was founded by King David I, brother of King Henry's wife Matilda. He travelled to England with her, when she first came to Romsey as a young girl, and afterwards resided for a while at the English court. He may well have been aware of the architectural plans for Romsey's new church.

When work was continued on the nave, a return was made to the type of clustered pier which is found in the chancel and the width of the bays was increased at the same time. After the first bay, the style is kept plain and simple with no further decoration of the arches or carved capitals, apart from one bay referred to below in the north aisle in the part used as a parish church.

Up to this point in the building, the distinctive warmly-coloured stone came from Quarr and other places on the Isle of Wight. The colder stone used for the west end is said to have come from the Bishop of Salisbury's quarry at Chilworth.

The West End and Later Improvements

The longest pause in the building seems to have occurred after the fourth bay of the nave was completed. Funds may have run low or work may have had to be completed first on adjacent convent buildings. It is likely that a temporary west wall was erected so that the completed part could be used for services. When work began again in the 13th century, fashions in architecture had changed and the last three bays of the nave are built in the Early English style with pointed arches and rounded capitals. Three fine lancet windows were inserted in the new west wall.

Proof that the masons began at the west end and worked eastwards, so as to leave the temporary west wall undisturbed for as long as possible, seems to be found — although not all experts will agree — in the distinct bend in the building line at this point and also by the slight miscalculation which meant that the arch which adjoins the last Norman bay had to be cut short in order to fit it in with the space left when the wall was removed.

24

South side of nave showing giant column c.1820

Apart from the change in style, an indication that further building work was in progress in the thirteenth century can be obtained from entries in the Close Rolls of King Henry III between 1251 and 1253. They record that he gave a total of 38 oaks to the abbey from the New Forest during that period. In one gift of sixteen trees it is specifically stated that they are for use in the building of the church.[5]

There were other presents from the king to the abbess, such as a tun of wine or a buck from the forest, but he exacted a return for his gifts. When the court came to Winchester to celebrate Christmas, as it did from time to time, all the towns around, including Romsey, had to share in the baking of bread; and for Christmas in 1250 the abbess of Romsey was commanded to provide fifteen pigs and vast quantities of eggs as a contribution towards the lavish celebrations.

Around 1300 the small Norman windows in the east end of the chancel were replaced by much larger ones in the Decorated style and the Lady chapel was rebuilt with windows of the same style. The archways of the Norman windows are still clearly visible on the outside.

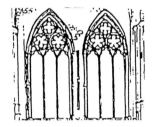

East windows

The Parish Church

The townspeople had been allotted the north aisle of the nave for use as their parish church. It was partially separated by screens from the body of the nave but must have been very dark and narrow. As the population of Romsey grew, it became too small to meet the needs of the parishioners and in 1403 they petitioned William of Wykeham, the bishop, for permission to enlarge it. For William of Wykeham, founder of Winchester College and New College, Oxford, a famous church-builder and patron of the arts, this was a project after his own heart. He granted a licence to the vicar and parishioners to pull down the north aisle and rebuild it on a larger scale, agreeing with them that their church was too confined and mean for divine service and commending their desire to make it larger and more beautiful.

The building probably took three years. The vicar, John Umfray, was granted a papal indult to be absent from his parish for that period during which he could study at a university or reside at the papal court. Clearly it was impossible to conduct services in the parish church while building was in progress; no doubt

Carved mouldings round 'Abbess's Door' adjoining south transept

27

arrangements were made for the parishioners to attend the convent mass instead.

The north wall of the aisle was pierced with arches and a new wall built further north in a line with the north wall of the transept (the footings for this wall, whose existence was already known, were uncovered only a few years ago when the north driveway was repaved). The extra aisle meant that the parish church now had a new nave which was not only broad but light and airy, as it was lit on its north side by large windows in the Perpendicular style which had now become the architectural fashion.

The size of these windows can be judged by mentally piecing together the surviving top part of one window and the bottom part of another. These (with others, since replaced) were clumsily re- inserted in the north wall when the new aisle was demolished after the dissolution of the abbey, and may be seen just to the east of the north door.

Around 1407, when the work was completed, the parishioners would have had a large and well-proportioned parish church available for worship. They would have been able to look through an archway (now replaced by a window) which pierced the west wall of the north transept, which then formed their chancel, and through another archway (nowadays blocked by the painted wooden reredos described on p.35) to the sanctuary in the eastern apse of the transept. This is the area now used as a choirboys' vestry but evidence that there was once an altar here on a raised stone step may be found in the height of cuttings in the stone for piscina and aumbry which are still visible in the east wall.

One other curious feature may be pointed out in the north aisle of the nave. The fourth bay is different from all the others, which are plain and simple. In this bay the ribs of the vaulting have a crenellated pattern, its western pier has double shafts all round and the capitals, unlike the others in the nave, are decorated. The reason for this display may be that the parish font stood here on exactly the same spot where a font (not now the main one) stands today. The additional decoration was a way of celebrating the place where new members were welcomed into the Church.

The parish church was known as the church of St.Lawrence. We have visualized its fabric from the time it was enlarged until the dissolution in 1539.

28

Let us turn briefly to its furnishings. We know that there was a chantry chapel within the church, built about 1475, for the Brotherhood of St.George (see below p.34). Two or three other brotherhoods are mentioned during this period which presumably had their shrines or altars. There were many other images of saints (including St.Anthony, St.Clement, St.Blaise, St.John and St.Erasmus). We hear of them because in wills of the time small sums of money are left (usually twopence in the coinage of the time) for lights to burn before one or more of them.

Even before the church was enlarged, Bishop Orlton in 1334 gave permission for mass to be celebrated on a portable altar before the image of St.Catherine. After the enlargement, one may imagine many more altars and the twinkling of lights from many lamps burning before the shrines of the saints.

The Exterior

Mention has already been made of the Saxon rood on the west wall of the south transept. Close to it, on the other side of the corner, is the elaborately carved doorway, commonly referred to nowadays as the Abbess's Door, but it would have been the main entrance to the church for the nuns as they came through the cloisters from the chapter house or refectory. It was badly damaged by the roof of a shed which stood there in Victorian times, but it has since been restored. The corbel courses for the cloisters are visible and show that the cloisters had an upper storey.

Running all round the church, above the window level, there is a corbel table or stone parapet, embellished with human faces and animal heads. Also, set on its own above the window in the west wall of the north transept there is a strange squatting figure holding a staff. It has given rise to a legend that the mason fell out with the abbess and took his revenge by portraying her in her privy. It is likely to have more in common with a sheila-na-gig (ancient fertility figure), such as is found on the corbel table at the exquisite little Norman church of Kilpeck (Herefordshire). On the outside of churches masons could let their imaginations rip, often

Sheila-na-gig

29

depicting grotesque monsters or the sins of the flesh to represent the frightening and evil world which was banished by the Church.

The western end of the south nave wall has no ashlar (cut stone) because some part of the domestic range of convent buildings was joined to it. To the south of the church, in what is now a private house, a timber roof survives which may have belonged to the refectory. It dates from c.1230. Excavations have given clues to the lay-out of some of the other convent buildings (see plan). The archway from the Market Place is on the site of the old abbey gatehouse.

On the north side of the church, a modern porch (1908) has been built on part of the site of the medieval porch. It faces the old parish churchyard which is now grassed over.

Flamboyant perpendicular window in north wall

Mouldings

Heads from corbel table

a.

b.

c.

d.

a: Palmette, 'Abbess's Doorway' (see p.45)
b. Rope, 'Abbess's Doorway'
c. Dogtooth, north doorway
d. Egg and dart - capitals

REFERENCES

1. An architectural description will be found in Pevsner & Lloyd. An analysis of the probable   building phases is made by G.H.Hearn, 'Romsey Abbey', Gesta 1975
2. P.A.Wellington, 'Good Queen Maud', LTVAS P&P no.3
3. Liveing p.49, discussed by Coldicott p.31
4. J.H.Harvey, The Medieval Architect, p.120
5. Henry III, Close Rolls, 1251-1253, p.295

CHAPTER THREE

PRE-REFORMATION PAINTINGS IN THE CHURCH

Four examples of painting survive and, quite apart from any artistic merit they may have, each throws some light on the history of the abbey and the way the church was used.

Wall Paintings in the Retrochoir

On the wall to the right of St.Mary's chapel in the retrochoir are some early thirteenth century wall paintings which were uncovered earlier this century. They relate a story in four medallions which would have continued further eastwards before the main part of the Lady chapel was demolished. They have trefoil and foliated ornamentation in the spandrels and are bordered at the base with a deep band from which there hangs some painted drapery.

The scenes in the roundels are badly defaced and two totally different interpretations have been suggested. Expert opinion now favours the conclusion that they portray incidents in the life of St.Nicholas, a popular medieval saint. Originally they were studied by Professor Tristram[1] who believed that they told the story of the Abbess Elwina whose vision at mass of a coming Danish raid caused the sisters to pack their treasures and flee to Winchester (see p.7). According to this interpretation, in the top left roundel a bishop or abbot celebrates mass; top right is Elwina's vision and an altar which has been set on fire; and bottom right shows the nuns saving their treasures which include the statue of a bishop. From traces of other decoration now obliterated, Professor Tristram concluded that the painting, which is in black, green and white ochres, formed part of a comprehensive scheme around the east end of the church and, although now much defaced, was originally of high quality.

Later this century, in 1975, some extensive conservation work was carried out. The paintings were removed from the wall on to panels of silk while the wall behind was cleaned of salts and a new lime plaster applied. The paintings were then replaced[2]. David Park (now Director for the conservation of wall paintings at the Courtauld Institute) assisted in this sensitive operation and made a fresh study of the paintings. He found some similarities with the twelfth century stained glass portraying the life and

32

miracles of St.Nicholas in Chartres Cathedral. In that case our top left roundel shows the saint's consecration as bishop of Myra (a supposedly miraculous event); the top right one portrays the saint in his bath on the day he was born and the legend that he was unharmed although the water boiled (hence the steam in the picture). The scene at the bottom right would then illustrate part of the legend of a Jew who set up a statue of the saint to protect his belongings (in spite of this he was burgled and in his fury he beat the statue, whereupon St.Nicholas appeared to the robbers and persuaded them to return the loot)[3].There are undeniably some similarities with the Chartres medallions, but due to the state of the paintings neither explanation can be accepted as correct beyond any shadow of doubt.

The framed picture of a kneeling priest painted on a wooden panel in the retrochoir

The original panel is 4'8" x 2'3", consisting of two or three planks, now badly split. This panel has been framed by oak battens of a later date. The painting is in poor condition, but it is possible to make out the subject and to see that the quality was once good.

A kneeling figure is portrayed. He is evidently a cleric from his tonsure and he wears a dark grey amice or cloak. His hands are upraised in prayer and touch a scroll with the words *Ihu fili dei miserere mei* (Jesu, son of God, have mercy on me). The background is a rich red curtain, stencilled in gold leaf with small petalled flowers and wolves' heads, evidently of heraldic significance; it is also strewn with large gilt five-pointed stars of gesso.

Experts on late medieval painting consider the panel to be late 15th century from the style of the lettering, and agree that the figure would be that of a donor, forming part of a much larger composition.[4] This was in fact the case.

The discovery of the panel can be tracked down to a day in February 1813 when the then vicar and churchwardens decided to open up the arches behind the high altar, which had been blocked up for centuries. Fortunately, there was a reporter on the spot: Dr. Latham, the antiquarian, was present and recorded in his notebook the exciting discoveries which were made that day.

First, some panels were removed which were painted with the Lord's Prayer, Creed and Ten Commandments. Behind these, the Commandments appeared again in older script on a screen behind. When this lettering was washed off, there was revealed the reredos which is now behind the altar in St.Lawrence chapel (see below). This was not the end of the story: when this altar-piece had been carefully removed, those present were amazed to find another huge board, even more ancient, attached to the frame behind. Only one figure remained visible on this: it was our kneeling cleric. It must have been in a better state of preservation than it is now because Dr.Latham describes the figure as a monk who is wearing 'a girdle consisting of two hempen cords having at the ends a tassel of gold knobs'. This has now almost worn away. He also describes a shield, already partly effaced, above the cleric's head. Of this shield, all that is now visible are two chevrons. They appear to have been the arms of William of Wykeham (two chevrons sable between three roses gules), possibly commemorating the help he gave in 1403 over the extension of the parish church (see above p.26) Possibly his figure appeared above the shield: Latham says that there were originally four other figures, two above and two below our kneeling priest, but now 'blank and black' and the whole panel, he recounts, was 'fastened to a very substantial oak frame mortised into the wall'.

It is possible to hazard a guess as to the identity of the cleric and the original position of the panel. A Brotherhood of St.George was in existence in Romsey by the middle of the 15th century and in 1475 Edward IV granted letters patent for the founding of a chantry of St.George within the parish church. In almost every will made in Romsey at the beginning of the 16th century a bequest is made to the Brotherhood, one of whose functions was to maintain a bede roll. This was a list of names of the dead for whom masses would regularly be said by the chantry priest. The chantry, like those which still survive in many cathedrals, would have been a small chapel, usually placed between two pillars of an aisle. This might well have been of wood, such as survives with a painted interior at Hexham Abbey in Northumberland[5]. Our kneeling cleric would have formed part of the south wall of such a chantry.

In 1866, when a Norman window was restored in the north aisle nearest to the north transept, shields bearing St.George's crosses were found painted on the soffit or under part of the colonnading formed when the north wall was pierced to add an extra aisle to the parish church in 1403. It is possible that the chantry of St.George was built within this arch of the colonnade.

The identification made[6] of the present chapel of St.George in the north choir aisle with the medieval chantry of St.George is not sustainable. The choir aisles always formed an integral and essential part of the nuns' church, being regularly used for their Sunday processions. The parish church, to which the chantry belonged, never extended eastward beyond the north transept. After the dissolution all side chapels were dismantled and were only restored for worship in comparatively recent times, when the northern chapel was probably called after St.George because of the tradition that there had once been a chantry of that name in the abbey. The chapel, however, is noteworthy for its medieval floor tiles which once covered the chancel floor.

Who then is the kneeling cleric? There is a record that a Thomas Wolsey Canonicus was ordained deacon in Romsey Abbey in 1480[7]. This is just the period of greatest interest in the chantry and the probable date of the panel. (Incidentally, this Thomas Wolsey has no known connection with the great cardinal of that name who was only born in 1471.) The name 'Wolsey' is derived from 'Wulfsige'='Wolf-Victory'. The heraldic wolves' heads may therefore have been a pun on the donor's name. At this time there were two or three canons or prebends appointed to the convent. They were often lay canons so this could explain why Thomas Wolsey was described as 'canonicus'. He may have served as the chantry priest: he was almost certainly a benefactor.

Chantry chapels were suppressed and their endowments confiscated in the first year of Edward VI's reign. Panels containing the Lord's Prayer and Ten Commandments were ordered to be put up in churches at about the same time, so it would be natural to make use of this large, redundant board for the purpose.

The wooden Reredos behind the altar in the north transept

The unblocking of the arches behind the high altar revealed not one treasure but two. The second was the wooden reredos which, as mentioned above, is now in St.Lawrence's chapel, although it was then at least half as large again as the screen which we see now. The top part consisted of an ogee arch enclosing a painting of the Lord in Majesty surrounded by adoring angels.

Part of south transept c.1825

The older script which had been painted directly over the figures was fairly easily removed, but when the lettering became worn and panels with fresh script of a later date were nailed on top, they failed to cover the whole reredos. The gaps above and below were therefore painted in oils to represent black and white marbling. In 1813 no satisfactory method was known for removing this oil paint, so the reredos was cut down to its present size and framed. It was restored by Professor Tristram in 1929 and placed in its present position to screen off the area now used as a choirboys' vestry from the rest of the chapel.

We are now left with a row of nine saints and below them a scene of the Resurrection. Christ, dressed in a red cloak over a white loin-cloth, is stepping from the tomb to the amazement of the guards. These soldiers are clad in English medieval plate armour and two of them are armed with poleaxes. On either side angels in white albs are swinging censers and to the left is the figure of the donor abbess with her staff, from whose mouth come the words *Surrecsit Dominus de sepulcro* (the Lord has risen from the tomb).

Experts have dated this screen to the period 1525-1530 and it clearly straddles medieval and renaissance styles. Pevsner describes it as 'bad but rare'. The figures have a medieval look, but the decorations and ornamented pillars belong firmly to the renaissance and cannot be earlier than Henry VII's reign. In any case, it was Henry VII who first made St.Armel (one of the saints depicted) popular in this country, having become familiar with his cult in Brittany. At the other extreme, the reredos must be earlier than the dissolution of the abbey in 1539 because it was commissioned by an abbess. We are almost certainly looking at the figure of the last abbess of the nunnery, Elizabeth Ryprose (1524-1539).

We can probably fine down the date of the reredos even further by looking at the choice of saints. What led the abbess to choose this rather strange assortment of characters from different centuries?[8] In a Benedictine nunnery it is not surprising to find St.Benedict in the centre with his sister, St.Scholastica, patron of nunneries, on his left.

37

With regard to the other saints, the first figure on the left of the board is St.Jerome, the Biblical scholar. He was perhaps venerated by Benedictine nuns because at one time he was leader of a group of Roman ladies who were drawn to an ascetic and studious way of life.

Next to Jerome is St.Francis. Earlier guide-books identified the small kneeling figure at his feet as St.Clare, but she cannot be a saint as according to the traditions of hagiography she would not have been depicted without a halo. She wears black and is holding a coral rosary. Originally there was gold on her head-dress and she looks like a prosperous widow.[9] It is possible that she is the Lady Giacoma di Settisoli, the wealthy widow of a Roman noble, who was the ministering Martha to the Franciscan brothers in the same way that Clare ministered to their spirit.

The two bishops (fourth and far right) cannot be identified with certainty, although one may be St.Swithun, patron saint of the diocese.

St.Armel (second from right), as we have seen, had been recently popularised by King Henry VII who believed he owed much to Armel's intercessions. This 6th century saint was supposed to have emigrated to Brittany from Wales, as Henry himself had done before he seized the throne of England. There is a statue of Armel in the Henry VII chapel in Westminster Abbey. It is uncertain why this saint is usually shown wearing armour and a chasuble, but the legend that he commanded a dragon to drown itself in the river Sèche is the reason why he is usually portrayed, as here, using his stole to tie up the dragon (depicted as small and insignificant and resembling a little pig).

We are left with only two saints unexplained: St.Sebastian (third from left) and St.Roche (third from right). The common factor between these two otherwise disparate saints is that both were invoked to intercede against plague. Here may be the clue to an almost exact date for the reredos: in 1526 Henry VIII cancelled a proposed visit to Romsey because of an outbreak of plague there, as recorded in a letter to Wolsey from Lord Sandys:

> The King to be at Winchester on the Eve of the Assumption and will spend there the time he intended to be at Romsey, where the sickness is.[10]

If the abbess was commissioning a reredos at this time, what could be more natural than to include the two saints specially invoked for protection against plague?

Sebastian, who was shot to death by arrows under Diocletian, is a well-known saint, but Roche (also known as Rock or Rocco) needs some explanation. He was born at Montpellier in the 14th century of a rich merchant family and became a hermit. He is said to have nursed plague sufferers until he caught the disease himself and retreated into a wood to die. The legend is that he was found by a dog who brought him some bread in its mouth and licked his sores until he was cured. He is often accompanied by a little dog with a bun in its mouth. Here he is depicted pointing to the plague sore on his leg.

Some older guidebooks stated that the reredos was painted by an Italian artist who had been working in Winchester cathedral under the direction of Bishop Fox and the myth has often been repeated. The only apparent evidence for this is that the bishop had some new mortuary chests made for the bones of the Saxon kings and saints which were said to be painted in quite an Italian style. While, as mentioned above, there is some renaissance influence in the painting of the pilasters on the Romsey screen, the soldiers are firmly English and medieval and the statement is quite unfounded.

It is extremely rare for a wooden reredos of this period to survive and we are fortunate that circumstances kept it hidden for three hundred years. It is not an object of beauty but it is interesting and unusual and brings to life for us the last decades of the abbey's existence. We can imagine the quaking terror of the nuns at the outbreak of plague and their exclamations of wonder as the huge painting was erected above the high altar. We can feel too the irony of their ignorance of the fate in store for them only a dozen or so years later when their convent would be closed and they, whatever their personal wishes, would be thrown back into the world. In the controversies that followed, the saints themselves would be banished from the church.

Other wall paintings

The eastern apse of the north transept, which once formed the sanctuary of the parish church (see above p.28), is now separated off from St.Lawrence chapel by the reredos just discussed. In its vaulting there is patterning

39

composed of crescents, stars and quatrefoils, and at the intersection of the vault the ribs are painted in alternate squares of red and white outlined in black. Also, on the pillar separating the vestry from the rest of the transept, there are traces of diagonal lines of red paint. Finally, on the pillars in the south choir aisle on each side of the treasury there are traces of horizontal bands of decoration on a white background.

None of this work is of very high quality but it reminds us of how much of the interior stonework in a medieval church would have been covered by painting and decoration. If it had all survived, we might find the result garish today, but to our forebears it brought life and colour into the building.

REFERENCES

1.   Prof. E.W.Tristram, *English Medieval Wall Paintings*, vol.III, p.190
2.   Mrs Diane Hargreaves kindly supplied this information
3.   A different version of this story is given in Etienne Houvet, *Chartres Cathedral*, Académie des Beaux-Arts,1930
4.   Letter from Dr. Clive Rouse
5.   Miss Anna Hulbert who carried out conservation work on the panel in 1991 kindly supplied this information
6.   Coldicott, p.62
7.   Liveing, p.247
8.   The identification of some of the saints has been disputed, but the list given is now usually accepted
9.   Description supplied by Miss Anna Hulbert who carried out conservation work on the reredos in 1992
10.   Letter to Wolsey from Lord Sandys, quoted Liveing, p.244

CHAPTER FOUR

PRE-REFORMATION MONUMENTS, CARVINGS AND RELICS

Medieval heads on top of a wooden screen (separating north transept from choir).

These fourteenth century carved heads of kings, abbesses and bishops from an old screen had been stored in a gallery where they were discovered and placed on a modern screen c.1880 by the then vicar, the Rev. E.L.Berthon. In accordance with Victorian fashion he used the screen to separate the chancel from the nave, but the heads are now probably back in their original position where they separated the parish chancel from the monastic church.

The heads are in trefoils with running foliage above. They cannot now be individually identified, but Berthon had new choir stalls made, with well-executed matching heads of monarchs, abbesses and bishops. On the north side they include Queen Victoria and Prince Albert. Berthon had demonstrated his nautical inventions to them (see chapter 11) and his own likeness faces them on the southern clergy stall.

Recumbent Purbeck marble effigy in south transept

This fine effigy of an elegant lady dates from c.1300. The recumbent figure, with a canopy over her head, is cut from a single block of Purbeck marble. For centuries it lay upside-down in the floor at the west end of the nave, no doubt to escape the iconoclasts of the 16th and 17th centuries. It was re-discovered early in the 18th century and placed in the recess below a handsome ogee arch of somewhat later date which was probably designed for an Easter sepulchre.

There has been some damage to the monument but the lady herself is intact. She wears a tight-sleeved loose robe which falls to the feet in folds but is held at the waist by belt and buckle. Her left hand grasps the cord which fastens her cloak at the shoulders, while her right hand holds a fold of her robe. She is wearing a wimple and her head rests on a cushion. Her pointed shoes rest on a lion or dog.

It is easier to say who this lady is not than to identify who she was. She is certainly neither royal nor an abbess, as she wears no crown and holds no pastoral staff. She was evidently a person of importance and probably was a benefactress of the abbey. During the 13th and 14th centuries Romsey abbesses were connected with some of the greatest families in the land, who indeed were often related to each other by marriage, and several famous heiresses have been suggested. Perhaps the strongest claim can be made out for Joan de Nevill, a great heiress whose widowed mother was abbess between about 1238 and 1244. It may have been in memory of her mother that Joan entered into an agreement with the Abbess Cecilia in 1244 by which she gave a caracute (about 100 acres) of land in 'la Lee' to come into possession of the convent 'in free and perpetual alms at her death'. In return the abbess agreed to appoint a chaplain to celebrate divine service for the souls of Joan and her ancestors and heirs for ever.[1]

Even if we knew the features of the person commemorated, this would not help in identification. Such effigies were not intended to be likenesses, although the costume is a clue to the dating. There were centres for carvings made from Purbeck marble which was a popular material for effigies at this period and, although the craftsmen were highly skilled, they used stock patterns and made no attempt at portraiture.

Purbeck marble is not a marble in the strict sense, but a dark conglomerate from the Isle of Purbeck which is capable of taking a high polish.

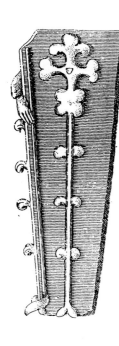

Tombstones of
abbesses

Three stone coffin lids of abbesses are preserved in the abbey. They date from the 13th and 14th centuries. One lid has been identified, although not with complete certainty. We know nothing of the identity of the other two abbesses and the slabs can only be dated approximately by comparing the style of carving with others elsewhere in the country of known date.

The most curious and most elaborate may also be the earliest. It is to be found in St.Ethelfleda's chapel. There has been some damage at head and foot of the stone but a beautiful foliated cross runs down the centre and the hand of the deceased abbess pushes up the coffin lid still clasping her staff of office. Its tip is in the mouth of a dragon or serpent (not included in the drawing).

The theme of the hand holding the pastoral staff is repeated on another coffin lid of which only the upper half has survived. This time a wide sleeve crosses the top of the lid and from it a hand emerges grasping a staff at right angles which runs down the centre of the stone. The lines here are quite simple and clear. Pevsner dates it as 13th century.

The third lid is tucked away near the south door. According to the Victorian historian, Charles Spence[2], it originally showed the outline of a lady with a

43

dog at her feet and a cross super-imposed, but this has entirely worn away. Round the edge was an inscription in doggerel Latin:

> *Abbatissa Johanna hic jacet humata ipsius animae Christus det praemia grata*

which Spence roughly translated as:

> *The abbess Joan here lies interred*
> *To her soul may Christ give reward*

The lettering too is almost obliterated and Spence was responsible for the new simple inscription of name and date which appears on the centre of the slab. He felt reasonably certain that this was the coffin lid of Joan Icthe, an abbess who died in the Black Death in 1349, or else of her successor, who was another Joan — Joan Gerveys — who died only three years later.

Two other tombstones, whose brasses have been torn away by past vandalism, probably also commemorated abbesses. One is the altar tomb, now in St. Mary's chapel. It has no inscription but the depression on the top, once filled with brass, suggests the outline of an abbess with her staff. (The heraldic shields on the side are modern additions.) The tomb once stood on the left-hand side of the chancel. A tombstone on the floor of the north side aisle similarly once contained a brass whose shape suggests the effigy of an abbess.

Carved stone heads

On the west window sill of the north transept are preserved the corbel heads of a king and a bishop and by the altar there is the head of a woman, possibly an abbess. There are good reasons to suggest that the king, who is portrayed with sharp eye and originally gazed down from the west gable of the church, is Henry III: the west front was completed during his reign with the

44

help of his gifts, and an identical crown appears on the thirteenth century gilt and bronze effigy on his tomb in Westminster Abbey.

The little row of four heads on the south-east pier of the tower is interesting: a similar group, surmounted by an identical form of palmette moulding, is to be found in the cloister at Tournus, France, dated c.1100, and may have been the model for the Romsey mason (The same moulding occurs in the elaborate carving round the 'Abbess's Door'.) There is also a large face above the giant columns on each side of the nave. There are heads where the Early English arches join the Norman, and a close search will reveal others.

Stone lamps or cressets

In the glass show-case at the west end of the church are two stone lamps, known as cressets. One contains two round cavities and the other, which is lozenge-shaped, contains four. They were discovered in the course of repairs during the last century, embedded with other rubble in a wall at the east end of the church. At the bottom of each cup there is a hole which held a stout wick. When the cressets were found, they still contained the charred remains of wicks and the tallow which was pressed round them

The flame from four such wicks together would produce a strong light. The cressets may have been used to give light to the masons while at work on the building or, more romantically, they may have been placed on ledges to light the night processions of the nuns from their dormitory into the church. In either case, they are undoubtedly of twelfth or thirteenth century date.

Embroidered cope/pall

On the wall in the north choir aisle there is an embroidered 'palla' or altar cloth formed from a cope, or possibly from two identical copes. The colours have faded but it was originally made of green brocaded velvet, decorated with golden six-pointed stars, and edged with a velvet, now buff-coloured, but which may once have been pink or crimson. This piece is embroidered with stylized plants and flowers.

The embroidery has been dated as late 15th century. There is no record of the nuns being engaged in embroidery in this late period and it has been

45

suggested that it was probably made in a commercial workshop.[3] The alterations may have been made after the dissolution when the abbey copes were no longer used.

As the history is lost, it has also been argued that the embroidery may only have been given to the abbey in the 19th century since it is not mentioned in the notebooks of the indefatigable antiquarian, Dr.Latham, who lived in Romsey until 1819. However, a guide-book of 1841 says that 'within the memory of persons yet living' it once had a further outer edging of cloth of gold.[4] This statement suggests that memories of it went back at least to Latham's time, but, if so, it is difficult to explain why he failed to mention it, except that it was being used as a vestry tablecloth and was in a poor state of repair. All that can be stated with certainty is that from this relic we can see an example of the kind of elaborately embroidered copes which priests would have worn at festivals in the abbey church. Some major conservation work on the embroidery was completed in 1983.

In the TREASURY there are two items of particular interest:

The Romsey Psalter

The psalter, from the style of the script and internal evidence, can be dated to the middle of the 15th century. It has become known as the Romsey Psalter but it was only acquired for the abbey in 1900 when it appeared in the catalogue of an antiquarian bookseller. He identified it as having originated in Romsey because three separate feasts of St. Ethelfleda are listed in the kalendar. The main festival is on October 23rd (a red letter day) but there are also feasts on 27th January and 10th March (black letter days) commemorating respectively her 'translation' and 'revelation'.

The psalter, however, has several other distinctive features which conflict with this view and have even led to the rejection of any Romsey connection.[5] That verdict goes too far as some association with Romsey is undeniable. However, it was apparently written for Franciscan use by someone connected with a Benedictine abbey and by the 16th century was undoubtedly in the possession of St. Mary's Abbey in Winchester. The arguments are given in full in Appendix Five. The psalter was examined and analysed by Neil Ker who was one of this country's greatest manuscript-scholars, and the latest edition of his work[6] summarizes the book as "written in England, apparently for Franciscan use ... in the vicinity of Romsey".

The Deed of Sale

Secondly, there is a document of which Romsey may justly be proud. It is the Deed of Sale, dated 20th February 1544, whereby the townspeople after the dissolution of the nunnery bought this great church from the Crown, together with a small area of land around it. The deed is sealed and signed with a great flourish by King Henry VIII himself, and the agreement is made with four local men, described as 'guardians', who act on behalf of the church. The small drawing within the initial letter seems intended to be a likeness of the king.

The one hundred pounds which was paid to the Crown was a large sum in the coinage of the day for a small town to raise in order to save the abbey church for parish use. One hopes that generous contributions came from those fortunate enough to be allowed to buy or lease the site and lands of the nunnery which were sold at the same time, but there is no record of this.

This transaction, agreed by the king because of the happy chance that the parish church was an integral part of the abbey church, saved this magnificent building from the wholesale destruction which was the fate of so many abbey churches after the dissolution. In many other abbeys (e.g. Shrewsbury and Leominster) the east end was demolished and only the nave, where the townspeople had worshipped, was left to be the parish church.

Medieval Paving Tiles

On the sanctuary floor of the eastern chapel in the north choir aisle (St.George's Chapel) there are preserved some of the fourteenth century encaustic tiles which once paved the chancel floor. Another six are to be found in the angle of a pillar base in the south choir aisle and more are

47

behind the curtain over the abbess's doorway. Similar tiles have been found at other places in the neighbourhood, such as Winchester, Netley, Beaulieu and St.Cross[7], and as far away as Great Bedwyn near Hungerford. Ancient kilns for baking such tiles have been found in other parts of the country and it is probable that there was a kiln in this vicinity.

On a base of red clay, a design was impressed by means of a stamp cut in relief. The hollowed-out designs were then filled with a whitish clay and the whole surface covered with a metallic glaze. Patterns include geometrical, decorative, legendary or historical designs. Some decorations are on single tiles, but sometimes four tiles are set together to make up a floriated cross, each tile containing one arm of it, either represented by a plain fleur de lys or by a more elaborate design which includes foliage and circles. There are also a number of single tiles which are decorated with stars, circles or flower petals.

In St.George's chapel there are some single tiles which appear to portray a knight templar; others show a mounted kingly figure at full charge; and there are many of a lion, statant dexter. Of particular interest, behind the central front tile (a moon over two stars), there is a larger tile with top corners removed which has a figure on horseback, possibly kingly, at full charge, and further back still a large, oblong tile, much defaced, which appears to have two mounted figures in conflict. One theory has been that they depict Richard I and the Saladin.

REFERENCES

1.   Liveing, op.cit.p.74
2.   C. Spence *Handbook to Romsey Abbey*, 1841 ed. p.96
3.   Coldicott, op.cit., p.85
4.   C. Spence, op.cit.p.58
5.   Coldicott, op.cit.p.69
6.   N.R.Ker & A.J.Piper, *Medieval Manuscripts in British Libraries*,
`   vol.4, pp.218-219
7.   An expert appraisal of the medieval floor tiles by Dr.A.Russel
        will be available in the forthcoming TVAT monograph on
        Romsey Abbey, ed.I.Scott, sponsored by English Heritage

CHAPTER FIVE

LIFE IN THE MEDIEVAL ABBEY

(AUTHOR'S NOTE: No book on Romsey Abbey would be complete without some account of the nuns who lived and worshipped here, but the details of their life, their properties, the administration of the convent and the circumstances surrounding the dissolution lie outside the scope of this book. Readers are referred to D.Coldicott, *Hampshire Nunneries* and H.Liveing, *Records of Romsey Abbey*, where these matters have been fully researched. This chapter largely summarizes their findings and footnotes are only given for material found elsewhere.)

The Rule of St.Benedict was made the established norm for monasticism in the time of King Edgar. In contrast with the ascetic extremes of the desert fathers in the east, the mark of Benedict's way of life was balance and moderation. The day was punctuated by seven short daily services, based on readings from the psalms, with a longer service in the night. St. Benedict's intention was that these daily offices should be balanced by periods for meditation and study and periods for manual work. His ideal was a Christian community which could be held up as a mirror to the world. Any guest who came to the monastery asking for hospitality must be cared for as if he were Christ[1], but the monks themselves were to remain within the cloister, undistracted by the world.

In his prologue to the Rule, Benedict said that he hoped it contained 'nothing that is harsh or burdensome'. It prescribed a life which, in its rules concerning fasting and silence, was not particularly austere. Nevertheless religious orders have never found it easy to maintain the high ideals of their founders. In the Middle Ages, even though there were always monks and nuns who were faithful to their vows and vocation, there were many factors at work which over the centuries undermined the ideals of St.Benedict and contributed to the gradual decay of the monastic houses. These will emerge as we look at life in the nunnery at Romsey under various headings.

The church worship

In addition to the daily offices, there were many celebrations of the mass. Bishop Woodlock in 1311 ordered a daily rota to be kept to ensure that at least eight nuns would be present at the Mass of the Blessed Virgin which was to be celebrated early in the morning so that those present would not be hindered from attending later sung masses[2]. The main service of the week, of course, was the solemn high mass with procession on Sundays.

In spite of all the changes to the church building since the Dissolution, it is still possible to see how it was carefully designed to accommodate the worship of a large Benedictine community. Its function was to provide: (i) a large choir for the recitation of the offices; (ii) a sufficient number of altars for all the resident priests to celebrate a daily mass; and (iii) a carefully arranged path for the processions.

There is archaeological evidence that the nuns' choir originally extended westwards down to the third bay of the nave. It probably only began at the crossing because the chancel was kept clear for the altar and large body of clergy who made up the presbytery. The nuns' choir was cut off by screens from the west end of the nave, the aisles and transepts. All the sisters would be in their places before the start of the Sunday procession (see above p.16). After processing round the retrochoir and out into the cloisters for a blessing of the convent buildings, they would come back into the nave of the church by the south-western entrance and pass through the doors on each side of the rood screen to take their places again in the choir. The procession was accompanied by chanting and incense with pauses for prayer at every altar.[3] It would have been an impressive sight.

Growth and decay over the centuries

From the Norman period onwards enough records survive to give a fairly full picture of the daily life of the nuns. Up to the early fourteenth century, in spite of some problems and abuses, the convent flourished under royal patronage, the great new church was built and there seems to have been no difficulty in the recruitment of nuns. In fact, in 1311 Bishop Woodlock decided that the abbey was overburdened with nuns and ruled that no more were to be admitted until numbers were back to normal. (He did not state what was 'normal' but it may well have been a hundred - the number of nuns whom King Edgar was said to have placed in Romsey Abbey.) In 1333 at the election of a new abbess ninety-one nuns were recorded as present, so the numbers had apparently been slightly reduced by then.

50

When the Black Death swept the country in 1349, the situation changed dramatically. Romsey Abbey seems to have been particularly hard hit. It is not known how many of the nuns perished in that year, but the plague swept away an abbess, a prebend and two vicars. There were several further outbreaks of the disease in the century which followed and the abbey never recovered from the blow. In 1478 the names of only eighteen nuns are recorded and although in 1501 the statutory number was stated to be forty, the number never again rose above twenty-five.

The nuns

Under the Norman kings the nunnery was a fashionable place, drawing recruits from the highest aristocratic and wealthy county families, and there seems to have been no lack of vocations from the genuinely devout. Unfortunately the standards inherited from Saxon times were not maintained. In the first place, a convent was considered the only alternative to marriage for a girl for whom, by reason of physical or mental defects or through lack of sufficient dowry, no suitable husband could be found. Secondly, because the nunnery took young children to educate them in the hope that the girls would later take the veil, guardians would sometimes place child-heiresses in a convent so that they could appropriate their fortunes for themselves. Finally, illegitimate children, widows or erring wives would sometimes be dumped there without being given any choice in the matter.

All nuns of the Middle Ages were well-born and in the Norman period were French-speaking. The English peasantry with their hard life of toil had neither education nor leisure for the religious life and could not afford even the minimum dowry expected for a nun's keep on taking vows. However, girls from such backgrounds could be accepted as lay sisters, keeping a simple rule and helping with the manual work of the convent.

In the later Middle Ages even the choir nuns were less educated than their Anglo-Saxon sisters had been, since formal education was not then considered an asset for well-born ladies. The offices were sung in Latin, but few nuns were well-versed in the language. In 1311, when the bishop sent injunctions in Latin to tighten the discipline of the abbey, he was obliged to send a translation into Norman French in order to make sure that they were understood.

The daily routine

The strict routine of a Benedictine abbey involved, as has been said, no great austerity, but the nuns must have found it hard to rise from their warm beds at 2 a.m., particularly on a cold winter's night, in order to go down to the draughty choir for about an hour to sing the offices of matins and lauds. It was the duty of one nun to make the rounds of the stalls with a lamp to check that all were present and that none had dozed off to sleep. After the service the nuns would return to their dormitory for another three hours' sleep before rising again at 6 a.m.

After the morning office of prime, the sisters met in chapter. They listened first to the martyrology and necrology (commemoration of the departed) and then to a chapter of the rule. After that, tasks were allotted, complaints were voiced, public confession of faults was made and any necessary business conducted.

A few hours each day were supposed to be devoted to work which might consist of reading, teaching or embroidery and, in summer, help with the hay-making or harvest. Compline at 7 p.m. in winter and 8 p.m. in summer was the last office of the day. After that, the nuns were expected to retire to bed, but a common temptation, at times when discipline was slack, was to sit up late in the warming house (the one room where a great fire burned) and indulge in gossip .

Boredom creeps in

These ladies of good birth who entered the convent had never lifted a finger to help in the home and so were unable to fulfil St.Benedict's ideal of balancing prayer with manual labour. They were equally ill-equipped to carry out his third ideal of spending time in study and meditation. Once the balance of St.Benedict's way of life was upset, even worship could become irksome. The often-repeated strictures of the bishops as they tried to maintain convent discipline have to be understood in the light of our knowledge that many of the women addressed were not nuns by choice and had no strong sense of vocation. Their foibles can then be understood.

The keeping of pets was evidently a compensation for those deprived of an outlet for their natural longings for love, affection and motherhood. In 1387 Bishop William of Wykeham accused them of taking birds, rabbits, hounds and 'suchlike frivolous things' into the church and paying more heed to them than to the offices.

Some of the nuns would slip out into the town to eat or drink with friends in houses or taverns; others would find excuses for journeys away from the convent to visit their families; others again would indulge in delicacies of food or finery in dress. The repeated rebukes on such matters show that the rules were more honoured in the breach than in the observance.

Dress

As early as 1138 a church council in England forbade nuns the use of furs. Vair (squirrel), miniver (white fur), ermine, sable, marten and beaver were explicitly listed (an interesting sidelight on furs commonly in use). It would be small wonder if, in the half-completed church, with icy winds whistling through the arches and draughts blowing the candle flames in all directions, the Romsey nuns ignored that injunction. They were supposed to dress in the black habit of their Order, so one wonders how Agnes Harvey was able to wear the red mantle (possibly fur-lined) which was left to her by the vicar in his will. About the same time (c.1500) she was accused of wearing her hair long, so she was guilty of vanity if of nothing worse.

Agnes was already a professed nun in 1478, although possibly only sixteen at the time, so she must have been nearly forty at the time of the accusation. However, she rose from being sub-sextoness in 1501 to chantress by 1523 and sub-prioress in 1526 (when her predecessor in the office was deposed on grounds of negligence in her duties), so it appears that in her later years she was considered to be a sober and responsible member of the community. Another council, in 1200, forbade 'black nuns' (the Benedictines) to wear such things as coloured headdresses, silver or gold pins, or silk girdles. In 1387 William of Wykeham was still repeating the same injunctions to Romsey: evidently the council's orders had been ignored.

Food and drink

The main meal was eaten around midday in the refectory while one of the sisters read from an edifying book. The nuns also took a quick 'breakfast', after prime, of bread and beer and a light supper after vespers. The quantities of beer drunk seem staggering to us - for monks the minimum allowance recorded was a gallon each a day[4] - but one must remember that (i) it was a very weak ale, (ii) no hot drinks were available and (iii) water was not normally fit to drink. In 1492 the nuns complained about the beer's quality.

The main course at dinner was very often a thick pottage eaten on trenchers of bread, but the nuns were allowed 'pittances' or extra small delicacies on the many feast days. In Lent the chief food was salt or dried fish, but the cellaress, who was responsible for the catering, provided almonds, raisins and figs to 'spice' the monotonous fare. Towards the end of the abbey's history, the system of communal meals began to break down: the nuns broke up into smaller 'households' which messed together, sharing their individual food allowances.

The enclosure

The many attempts by the authorities over the centuries to preserve the peace and privacy of the cloister, which in theory nuns should never leave except in exceptional circumstances, met with little success. One of the ways by which a nun might slip out unnoticed into the town was through a door which separated the nave from the parish church. By this route a nun could reach the market place and avoid the beady eye of the portress at the abbey gate. To prevent this, orders were given that this door must be kept locked and bolted.

Chatter and gossip were a recurring temptation in a world in which privacy was almost unknown. There seems to have been a kitchen window which looked on to the market place or other public area for an injunction of 1507 orders the kitchen window to be provided with a lock and key to prevent the nuns holding converse with lay people through the window. The bishops fought a losing battle against the strict rule of enclosure and it is clear from their injunctions that they were forced to reach compromises which relaxed this rule so long as certain conditions were met: e.g. Archbishop Peckham ruled that nuns were not to go out *without a companion*; also, they were not to visit taverns or eat and drink in any house in the town of Romsey either on *leaving or returning to the convent*[5]. In other words, it is taken for granted that there are occasions when nuns have permission to leave the cloister.

Serious scandals

There were a few offences recorded which were far more flagrant than the infringements of the Rule referred to above, although they were spread over many centuries and were probably no more or no worse than in other religious houses. The earliest concerned the absconding or abduction of King Stephen's daughter, a twelfth century abbess. Her story is pathetic and the extent to which she was blameworthy is debatable. It is told on page 123.

In 1315, another scandal arose over the mysterious death, a few months after her election, of the abbess Alice de Wyntershull who was said to have been poisoned. There was evidently some scandal involved but there were attempts at the time to hush it up and the circumstances are obscure.

There were a few cases where nuns were accused of unchastity, and there is the strange story of Margaret Poyns, a nun in the fourteenth century, who was excommunicated for 'laying violent hands on the vicar in church'. She was eventually absolved, but we have no other details about this extraordinary scene.

The worst scandals occurred in the last half century of the nunnery's existence, when it had sunk both in numbers and reputation and when all too much justification was provided for its final suppression. The trouble started with Elizabeth Brooke who was elected abbess in 1472 and afterwards confessed to perjury and adultery (see below). The convent seems to have been thoroughly demoralized after that and, although its last two abbesses were apparently blameless, its reputation by then had suffered beyond repair.

Education in the abbey

Children of royal or aristocratic birth were educated in the abbey. As well as Henry I's future queen and her sister, we hear of King John's daughter, Joanna, who was taught by the nuns, although she lived nearby in his hunting lodge in the care of a governess. Small boys are also mentioned among the pupils. However, the education, at least in the later period of the nunnery, seems to have been fairly haphazard. In 1502, when there were were 26 nuns in the convent, Anne Westbroke (who was later elected abbess) is described as mistress of the school, so some teaching evidently continued right to the end. Bishops, trying to exercise some discipline, had frequently to order that the children were not to sleep in the dormitory with the nuns. Their boarding fees were one source of income for the nunnery but, in view of the low state of education of the nuns themselves, the teaching was probably fairly elementary. They would learn to read and sing and follow the services. Otherwise the aim was mainly to teach good morals, good religion and good housecraft.

In Anglo-Saxon and Norman times nunneries were noted for their beautiful embroidery and in its early years Romsey Abbey may have been in the forefront. King Athelstan gave a stole, which survives, to the shrine of St.Cuthbert at Durham. On it are embroidered the words (in Latin), *Elfled had me made for the pious Bishop Frithestan*. Elfled was the wife of Edward the Elder whose daughter Elfleda was the first abbess. She is likely to have shared in the skill, if not in the work. Embroidery probably remained an occupation of the nuns, even though standards dropped in later centuries.

Latin remained the accepted language of learning, but although, as we have seen, the future Queen Matilda had been well schooled in it, the women of the later Middle Ages were less literate. So far as we know, nuns never copied or illuminated manuscripts in the way the monks did.

Probably many girls passed from being pupils to becoming novices; they needed only to be sixteen when professed so, if they had entered as the result of family pressure, it is not surprising that some of them later complained that they had been forced unwillingly to take the veil.

A Puzzling Contradiction

Although standards after the Norman period undoubtedly fell, it would be an over-simplification to picture them as totally ignorant and untalented. There is a document of 1243 which witnesses to the existence of an apparently well-known workshop for religious images in Romsey at that date which was capable of producing carvings on a large scale. To the best of my knowledge, it has been overlooked by previous historians of Romsey and its abbey. It is an order from the king for *a large and beautiful image of the Virgin and Child with a canopy 18 ft. in width*. The figures are to have wooden crowns, with alternate silver gilt crowns set with precious stones for use at festivals. The order was given through the Winchester diocese for the work to be carried out at Romsey; carriage was then to be arranged to Westminster where the carving was to be a gift from the king to the abbot and monks. Orders for two sets of episcopal mitres, slippers, rings and croziers for the king's and queen's chapels are also included in the royal command.[6]

In the event, the whole order was later cancelled, but the fact of the existence of such a workshop in a small place like Romsey is intriguing. Its reputation must have been outstanding to make carriage of such a large image to Westminster worthwhile, and it seems probable that some similar work of art, with which the king was familiar, had already been made for the abbey church. It is hard to believe that the workshop was not in some way connected with the nunnery. The town of Romsey was developing from the 'vill' described in Domesday, entirely owned by the abbess as lord of the manor and consisting of a few hundred souls. Through the expansion of the wool trade some of its citizens were already emerging as prosperous merchants, but it is exceedingly unlikely that at that period there was any artistic centre in the town entirely separate from the abbey, even if its involvement was limited to providing patronage and facilities. Unfortunately, there is no corroborative evidence to throw light on the matter but there may have been an interest in the arts and culture of which we are unaware.

Administration

Even under an efficient abbess the running of such a large and complex community would have been complicated: in the hands of an incompetent one it could cause chaos.

Although at the time of the dissolution Romsey was the sixth richest nunnery in the country, on average the nunneries had only half the wealth of the men's houses. In spite of royal patronage, there were frequent financial problems. The abbey had considerable lands and income from rents, but the properties were split over four counties which cannot have made for efficient management. Income came partly from rents and tithes, partly from sums due from courts, fairs, mills and woods, and partly from payments from boarders or gifts. Stewards were sometimes dishonest and repairs to the many buildings were costly. In 1502 the state of the roofs of chancel and dormitory were such that 'if it happened to rain the nuns were unable to remain either in quire at time of divine service or in their beds'. In 1351, after the Black Death, the abbess had to appeal to the bishop for help because the convent was reduced to such a state of poverty.

Apart from repairs and the day-to-day costs of the nunnery and its servants, there were taxes and heavy legal costs, as well as almsgiving and pensions to be paid out. The bishops requested regular accounts to be submitted but they were often not forthcoming. The religious training hardly fitted the abbess for such a task or to undertake the oversight of officials to whom the account-keeping might be delegated.

The abbesses

The king's permission had to be sought before the election of a new abbess, and a fine paid to him after the election. The abbess in Norman times usually came from a well-known, noble family to whom the convent would look for support and patronage.

The abbess was 'lord of the manor' with all its rights and duties. She was a great lady and expected to be treated as one. She had her own lodgings and oratory and her own servants, and was expected to entertain the king and his entourage on occasion, to give hospitality to other local landowners and herself to make frequent journeys on the abbey's business. Not surprisingly she frequently succumbed to the temptation to behave autocratically in the convent.

Alice Walerand (1268-1298) was connected with the most powerful families in the country. Archbishop Peckham wrote to her on two occasions in an attempt to curb her autocratic behaviour. Among his injunctions he enjoined her to remove two stewards whom she had appointed against the wishes of the convent; she was not to keep pet monkeys or more than one dog; she must not have more than two maid servants; she was not to fare splendidly while her nuns went short; she must elect a nun to accompany her as her chaplain, and she must submit annual accounts to the convent. The archbishop endeavoured to rebuke her as her spiritual father:

know that thou art not mistress of the common goods, but rather the dispenser and mother of thy community, according to the meaning of the word abbess....And because thou hast been wont to do much according to the prompting of thy own will, we adjoin to thee three coadjutresses of laudable testimony ...in such wise that thou shalt in no manner concern thyself to pursue any business without the three.[7]

How far the headstrong Alice heeded these injunctions it is difficult to know.

Abbesses were frequently tempted to make unauthorized payments from the convent funds by using the common seal without consulting the rest of the community. Bishop after bishop writes to order that the seal be kept under several locks to which other nuns must hold the keys. William of Wykeham went so far as to order that the seal must be kept under seven locks and that no letter might be sealed without first being read to the whole convent.

In some ways the nunnery suffered even more when the abbess was weak and incompetent than when she was autocratic. In the final decades before it was closed, the abbey had fallen in reputation and status and no longer numbered distinguished women amongst its abbesses.

Elizabeth Brooke (1472-1502), after six years as abbess, confessed to crimes of adultery and perjury and resigned. Astonishingly, the sisters then re-elected her: she must have had a powerful personality. The bishop apparently disapproved, but had to accept the right of the nuns, confirmed by King Edgar's charter, to elect an abbess from their own community. As token of his displeasure, he forbade Elizabeth the use of her pastoral staff, symbol of her authority. With her position thus undermined and scandals of financial mismanagement persisting, discipline in the nunnery seems to have broken down badly after her re-election.

Unfortunately, she was followed by Joyce Rowse (1512-1515), the ex-kitchener, who was another disaster, chiefly remembered for her greed. She had to be warned not to entertain any of the clergy in her lodgings, and to avoid drinking and eating to enormous excess. She eventually resigned.

Although we hear no criticism of Joyce's two successors, Anne Westbroke who had been mistress of the school, and Elizabeth Ryprose, by then the last pages of the convent's history were being written.

The Dissolution of the Abbey

The troubles which beset the religious houses in the final years of their existence gave Henry VIII the excuse he needed for their closure, but many other factors were involved as well. Protestant ideas had filtered through from the Continent. Henry disliked the reformed teaching, but, impatient for his divorce, had broken with the pope and declared himself supreme head of the Church in England. He was greedy too for the wealth of the monasteries and in 1536, using various scandals as a pretext, he closed the smaller ones, where numbers had already declined, and confiscated their property. The inmates were transferred to larger monasteries or were pensioned off. For a time the king was inclined to spare the larger houses, and the abbey, in the hope of legalizing its position, asked him to confirm its charters and manorial possessions.

During 1538 Abbess Elizabeth Ryprose accepted that the writing was on the wall and did her best to provide for the abbey's servants and officials by arranging pensions and annuities. Under Thomas Cromwell, the king's agent, visitors toured the country to persuade the remaining houses to surrender or dissolve themselves by agreement. This pressure, accompanied by some disgraceful pillaging of shrines, including that of St. Mary's Abbey at Winchester, induced most convents to dissolve themselves voluntarily. In such cases pensions were granted to the abbess or prioress and her sisters. Life was easier for the monks because many became parish priests, or, where there had been monastic cathedrals, the abbot and monks continued as the new secular dean and chapter. What happened at Romsey is obscure. Even the precise date when the abbey was suppressed is unknown although it appears to have taken place in the spring of 1539. It is thought that there was some resistance because there is no record of any pensions being paid and that was unusual. What became of the abbess and of all but one of her 25 sisters remains a mystery.

The nun Jane Wadham

Jane is the only nun in the convent at the time of the Dissolution whose later history is known. She had entered the nunnery at a young age in 1523 and was later joined by her sister Katharine. They were cousins of Queen Jane Seymour. Jane married the abbey chaplain and receiver, John Foster, in spite of the king's disapproval of clerical marriages and of an ex-nun breaking her vow of chastity. At a subsequent commission of enquiry she declared that she had been forced by threats and machinations of malevolent persons to become a regular nun, but had always protested against it and therefore considered herself free from her vows. Jane and John's daughter married the son of Sir Francis Fleming, owner of Broadlands, and became an ancestress of the St.Barbe family whose memorial is in the south transept.

REFERENCES

1. Rule of St.Benedict, chap.53
2. Woodlock, *Register*, folio 153
3. F.H.Crossley, *The English Abbey*, p.62
4. Coulton, *Medieval Panorama*, p.274
5. Peckham II, pp.664-665
6. *Close Rolls* 27 Henry III, Pt.I, 1243 AD, Translation:

> *Order given to the guardians of the Winchester diocese for them to arrange to have made at Romsey a large and beautiful image of the Virgin and Child, with a canopy 18ft. in width, with very beautiful wooden crowns to fit Mother and Child, which may be removed and replaced, and with alternate silver gilt crowns to the value of 10 marks, set with stones, which similarly can be removed and replaced on solemn festivals. They are also to arrange for the same sculpture to be conveyed to Westminster as a free gift from the king to the abbot and monks of Westminster.*

> *Furthermore, they are to arrange for the making of two sets of episcopal mitres, two pairs of slippers, two episcopal rings with sapphires, and two croziers, to be placed in the king's chapel and the queen's chapel so that they will be ready on the arrival of the king in England. When the king knows the cost of the items ordered, he will arrange for their payment.*

7. Peckham II, pp.658-659 and III, 805-806

CHAPTER SIX

THE CHURCH AND THE NUNNERY

Supervision by the Bishops of Winchester

Occasionally the pope became involved in the affairs of the convent, but normally its oversight was the responsibility of the diocesan bishop. It was his duty to make periodic visitations in person or through a representative to examine the state of the abbey and question each nun individually. Afterwards, if shortcomings were found, injunctions would be sent to the abbess listing the matters which required reform. When the see of Winchester was vacant in 1284, Archbishop Peckham carried out the visitation himself and during a later interregnum a commissioner was appointed from Canterbury.

Some bishops held other offices as servants of the crown and neglected the affairs of the diocese, but many took their responsibilities seriously. Unfortunately their injunctions often remained unheeded and had frequently to be repeated by their successors. Bishop Woodlock (1305-1316) had previously been prior of St.Swithun's, understood the monastic scene and was not distracted by involvement with affairs of state. He proved to be a fair-minded diocesan but he could be stern in his rebukes when he found laxity in the religious houses. He strove to tighten their discipline and the translation of his injunctions into French, referred to in the previous chapter, which he ordered to be read out in the chapter of Romsey Abbey, was made to ensure that no sister could make the excuse that she had not understood them.

Two centuries later, the diocesan was Bishop Fox. He was a genuinely pious man but for many years had been occupied in affairs of state in the office of Lord Privy Seal. When he retired from royal service in 1516 he took up his duties as bishop of Winchester and was determined to reform the diocese which had suffered from his absenteeism. He saw that at the root of the Church's malaise lay the low level of education of the clergy and he devoted much wealth and energy in an endeavour to raise the standards. He founded Corpus Christi college where the Fathers of the Church were studied, rather than medieval commentaries, and the renaissance spirit of humanism and enquiry was encouraged in place of medieval ignorance and superstition.[1]

In particular, he was concerned at the laxity of the Benedictine convents in his diocese where again lack of education was in part its cause. He made a free translation of the Benedictine Rule into English (by then the common language of the nuns), not only making Benedict's words applicable in gender to the nunneries but expanding the saint's exhortations in his own homely and graphic style. In his own words, his aim was to translate *into our moder's tongue, commune playne, rounde Englishe, easy and redy to be understande.*[2]

Thus, from Chapter 64 of the Rule on the qualities required in an abbot, St.Benedict's measured Latin,

> *Let him not be turbulent or anxious, overbearing or obstinate, jealous or too suspicious, for otherwise he will never be at rest.*[3]

becomes in Fox's version, as quoted by Barry Collett,[4]

> *She shall not be full of hastiness, troubelous, nor of sour mood, or displayant countenance, she shall not be importune, or intolerable nor obstinate, nor self-willed, she shall not be entangled with jealousy, nor be too much suspicious, for such a person is never in quietness, nor never takes rest.*

In an earlier century he might have been the man to revitalize the religious houses as the spiritual powerhouses of the Church, but his reforming zeal came too late to halt the decline which contributed to their suppression.

The Prebends[5]

The royal founders of the nunnery appointed prebends or canons to provide it with clergy and to be resident dignitaries with stalls in the church and full voting rights in chapter. For their support they were allocated revenues from other well-endowed parishes where they were the rectors and in turn appointed vicars to carry out the parish duties.

At Romsey there were originally three prebends, but in time through a process of rationalization and the need to divert some of their revenues to the needs of the nunnery there remained only one. Some of the tithes and rents were from the local parish of Timsbury but some from as far away as Edington and Immer in the Salisbury diocese and from Sydmonton in the north of Hampshire.

The original intention was that the prebends of the convent, like the canons of a cathedral, should live together in the close, but as land everywhere increased in value, the income of prebends and canons grew and the office became a much sought-after preferment. The pope often had his own candidate whom he wished to reward or sometimes the king might petition him for a prebend on behalf of a favourite royal clerk. Since the canons could pay clergy to carry out the priestly functions required of them, it was not even necessary that they themselves should be ordained. Increasingly the holders of the office became non-resident or even foreigners who held other offices in plurality.

Solomon de Roffe, an early prebend, is probably to be identified with a person of the same name who was heavily fined in 1290 for being involved in homicide, corruption and extortion. At about the same period, Archbishop Peckham wrote to the abbess ordering her to keep another prebend, William Schyrlock, out of the convent because of his scandalous behaviour:

> *(He) leads a very disreputable life ... disturbs the nuns so that they are unable in the cloister and monastery to recreate themselves by reading and praying as is proper to the honesty of religion; with secular women too ... he holds suspicious colloquy in corners of the church ...*[6]

Fortunately, some prebends had a better reputation: not long after Schyrlock, Prebend John de Romesey, probably from the family of that name who were substantial landowners in Hampshire and Somerset, made over some of his property to the abbey soon after his appointment.

The Vicars

Unbeneficed clergy, appointed by the prebends, continued to look after the parish church until 1321. In that year on 9th September Bishop Asser, with the consent of the abbess and prebends, appointed a perpetual vicarage in the prebendal church of Romsey and instituted Henry de Chilmark as the first vicar.

A deed was drawn up in the following year which set out in full the provision made to support the vicar and his successors. He was to be given from the abbey a daily corrody or allowance of food and drink, equal to the portion of two nuns. He was also to receive tithes of flax, hemp, apples, pigs, cows, milk, cheese, calves, colts, pigeons, charcoal, sales of produce, and eggs, together with two cartloads of hay per annum. Other fees which he would receive and his own responsibilities for expenditure were also spelt out in detail. By 1373 these complicated allowances in kind were commuted, under Bishop William of Wykeham, to an annual payment of 18 marks a year.

Before the endowment of the vicarage we have no knowledge of the individual clergy who were actually shepherding the flock in Romsey, but from 1321 onwards in spite of considerable gaps in the official records it is possible to compile a fairly accurate list. In one instance the name of the vicar is only known because he witnessed a will and signed himself with the title, Vicar of Romsey.

From the long list of incumbents between 1321 and the suppression of the nunnery, many are known to us only by name but a few leap from the page and take on life from some scrap of information which has survived.

Henry de Chilmark's successor was Nicholas de Botelston (in other words, 'Botolph's Town' or Boston in Lincolnshire). He was a man of substance but for reasons unknown he owed the Dean of Lincoln the very large sum of £100 which in default of payment was to be levied on his goods and chattels in the county of Southampton.[7] He was the vicar upon whom the nun, Margaret Poyns, 'laid violent hands' in the church, which caused her to be excommunicated for a time (p. 55). The cause of the outburst is not related so we do not know whether the vicar was blameworthy. He died in the Black Death in 1349. The same pestilence carried off his unfortunate successor, William de Bures, who was appointed in July of that year and was dead in September. It is believed that in Hampshire alone about two hundred clergy perished from this pestilence.

The next vicar, John de Minstede, fared better and remained for more than twenty years. He was another wealthy man and left the abbey a considerable legacy of ploughland, meadow and wood as well as property in the town. He was followed by John Folyot, apparently a quarrelsome character because he twice fell out with the abbess, Isabella de Camoys. On the other hand, she had already held office for twenty years and was to continue as abbess for twenty more, so she may have been an authoritarian who liked her own way. Their first cause of dispute was when he refused to follow the time-honoured Palm Sunday tradition by which the palms were blessed at the nuns' high altar before the abbess and vicar joined in procession together. He may have felt that the nuns' choir was out of sight of his own congregation in the north aisle or else that the blessing of the palms should be his own prerogative. William of Wykeham, the bishop, was obliged to intervene and ordered Folyot to abide by the established custom.

The following year he had a further disagreement with the abbess over a question of repairs to a chapel on the north side of the parish church.[8] Thomas Eggesworth, the priest appointed to investigate the Palm Sunday dispute, became the next vicar, but it is not clear whether Folyot resigned as a result of the ill-feeling he had stirred up.

We have already met John Umfray who became vicar about the year 1400 (p.26) in connection with his absence from the parish for three years while the church was being enlarged. A Joan Umfray is listed in the convent at this time and was probably his sister.

We have a glimpse of John Greene (1464-1482) on the re-election of Abbess Elizabeth Brooke (p.55) following her resignation after scandals about her earlier life had come to light. It is recorded that three sisters were sent to announce the result of the election to the abbess who was waiting in a certain ground-floor parlour within the dwelling house of Master John Greene, vicar of the parish church. His house was evidently within the abbey precincts. He is described as a Bachelor of Divinity and eventually resigned as vicar on being appointed a prebendary. As he seems to have been a prominent churchman, he may be the same John Greene who for four years before his appointment as vicar had been headmaster of Winchester College.

In 1501 a nun, Emma Powes, was accused of incontinence with the vicar who was Richard Sclater. Nothing else is known of this man and possibly the scandal caused his resignation. His successor, Thomas Nayle, behaved more discreetly but was so charmed by the vain Agnes Harvey who was proud of her long hair (p.53) that he bequeathed her his red mantle and tapestry coverlet.

Finally, how revealing would have been the memoirs of John Newman (1519-1546) whose incumbency spanned all the troubled years during which the nunnery was swept away. In 1523 he celebrated the mass for the guidance of the Holy Spirit in what was to be the last election of an abbess of Romsey. He survived the pestilence which raged in the town in 1526. He must have been present about that time at the dedication of the great wooden reredos which Abbess Elizabeth Ryprose had commissioned. In 1530 he witnessed the will of a parishioner who left money for a vestment to be made for St.Antony's altar.[9] It stipulated that it should be as good or of equal value as a vestment lately given by one Sam Shepherd (an early example of keeping up with the Jones's!) Within a decade after that he witnessed the nuns' departure and had to adapt himself to the new ways of worship imposed by royal command. He had to swear allegiance to the king as Defender of the Faith in place of the Roman pope. With heavy heart he must have seen many items of beauty destroyed in the church. By this time he was an old man and sick, but he would have shared in the day of rejoicing in 1544 when the king finally signed the deed by which the abbey church became the property of the people of the parish and its future was assured as their place of worship. He lingered on for another three years, but died in 1547, leaving a Church where the old order had vanished and new problems and new challenges awaited his successors.

REFERENCES

1.   W.W.Capes, *Bishops of Winchester* pt.II, pp.75-79
2.   Liveing, p.227
3.   Justin McCann (transl.), *Rule of St.Benedict*
4.   B. Collett, *Monastic Studies* p.217 (Headstart 1990)
5.   Fuller accounts of the prebends are to be found in:
      a. Coldicott, p.55
      b. Moorman, op.cit. pp.96-98
      c. Arch.Journal LXXIV (1917)

6.   Peckham III, p.929
7.   Patent Rolls, 24th June 1347
8.   Liveing, p.169
9.   Tudor Wills, *Blosse* (Hants Record Office)

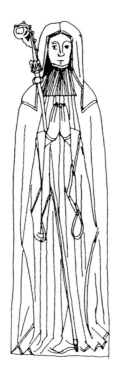

A Benedictine Abbess

CHAPTER SEVEN

THE CHURCH: INTERIOR CHANGES

The abbey church has seen many changes to its interior since the dissolution of the nunnery. Some were made for doctrinal reasons, others have been in response to the practical requirements of maintaining a large parish church in a small town.

I. CHANGES FOR DOCTRINAL REASONS

After the dissolution: the church physically contracts

The swift demolition of the lady chapel after the dissolution was probably due more to doctrinal reasons — ridding the church of a superstitious cult of the Virgin and the saints — than to the desire to avoid the expense of keeping it in repair. However, once the nuns' church had become the parish church with more than enough space for all its needs, the extension to the old parish church could also be swept away and the wall of the north nave aisle became again the outer wall of the church (see p.28).

Reform under King Edward VI

During the brief reign of the boy king, Edward Seymour the Protector and Archbishop Cranmer under the influence of Protestant ideas ordered the removal of all images, relics, vestments and chantries and also of all screens and partitions. They believed that the screen created a barrier between lay people and God, as though the clergy alone could obtain God's favour on behalf of his people. To the reformers it represented the veil of the temple which had been torn down by Christ and should no longer have a place in Christian worship. The idea of the people and clergy forming one body in worship was reinforced by the introduction of a prayer book in English which all could follow.

Catholicism restored under Queen Mary

When Mary, a fanatical Roman Catholic, ascended the throne, many of these reforms were reversed and vestments and other usages were restored, but too much had already been destroyed to allow a complete return to the old ways.

The Elizabethan Settlement

Most people welcomed the accession of Elizabeth whose settlement allowed for compromise and a degree of diversity. Even so, Thomas Chester, an ex-Marian priest who was vicar of Romsey in 1561, was accused of conducting a papistical burial because he had brought *a corpse into the church with candles and tapers ... and had suffered his parishioners to ring None on our Lady's Even, which was no Holy Day.*[1]

A year or so earlier an injunction had been issued requiring every church to replace its altar with a communion table (normally free-standing in the chancel) and to cover medieval wall paintings with the texts of the Lord's prayer, creed and decalogue. This is exactly what happened in Romsey: when the painted wooden reredos, now in the north transept, was discovered in the last century, it was found painted over with the creed; one lot of lettering was removed and even more ancient lettering discovered underneath. This earlier lettering probably dates back to the reign of Elizabeth.

We do not have any churchwardens' accounts from the period, but a typical record from another parish reads:

> *Timber for communion table.........................6s.*
> *Mending pavement where altar stood..........2s. 8d.*
> *To painter for writing scripture..................3s. 4d.*[2]

The injunction was repeated in a canon of 1604, so one imagines that churches which had failed to carry out the first injunction were obliged eventually to fall into line. Altars returned to the east end and were railed off to prevent them from desecration in the time of King Charles I's archbishop, William Laud. The position of the Holy Table, symbolizing differing views on the sacraments, remained a sad cause of controversy -- and probably of bewilderment to the man in the pew -- for many years. Here is a vivid description of a typical situation in a village church circa 1635.

... the fiercest controversy raged around the position of the Lord's Table. By the canon it should have been kept against the east wall, but for the Communion it might be brought down into the nave. It was, however, a heavy piece of furniture, and in many churches it was left permanently in the middle of the aisle. Here it became a resting-place for hats. Vestry meetings sat around it. Churchwardens wrote their accounts upon it. Latecomers even sat upon it for the sermon. There was much to be said in favour of Laud's new rule that it must be removed to the east end and reverently railed in, and that all who wished to communicate must kneel at the rails. But old-fashioned folk, who had never received the Communion anywhere but in their own pews, naturally disliked and distrusted this innovation. The result was absolute deadlock. The vicar refused to come outside the rails. The people refused to go up to them. He threatened to present them before the Archdeacon for withdrawing from Communion. They threatened to indict him at the next assizes for withdrawing Communion from them. And so the miserable squabble dragged on, causing continual bad blood and bitter feeling.[3]

Puritans, Civil War and the Commonwealth

The swings of ecclesiastical policy begun under the Tudor monarchs were to be followed by another great upheaval which nearly destroyed the Church of England's claim to be a true part of the holy catholic Church. Puritan influence had been growing throughout the country. With the overthrow of the king and the establishment of the Commonwealth (1648), a presbyterian form of government was imposed on the Church. Bishops were abolished and a new Directory of Public Worship replaced the Book of Common Prayer.

When civil war broke out in England, the vicar of Romsey was the scholarly Anthony White, M.A. of Corpus Christi, Oxford. He had become vicar in 1637 following the emigration to New England of Joseph Avery whose story is told on page 126. White was a high churchman and must have viewed with unease the spread of puritanism and the growing antagonism to the royalists.

One of the main causes of complaint among ordinary people was not religious but political. They objected to the illegal levy by Charles I for 'ship-money'. Romsey itself was instructed to raise £30 to this end in 1635. The money was ordered to be delivered to the Swan Inn by 20th October but by that date the small community was still 4s. 9d. short of the total.[4] Much resentment against the levy was felt in the town which already strongly supported parliament and favoured the puritans. Its citizens were largely artisans and small traders, many of them involved in the clothing industry which suffered from chronic depression. It was among such communities that dissent flourished. A survey of the population, taken a little later in the century (1676), showed a remarkably high proportion of dissenters in the town: there were 777 Non-conformists, three Papists, and 1070 Anglicans[5].

In the civil war it was Romsey's misfortune to be virtually on the borderline between the eastern half of the country, held by the parliamentarians, and the western which was loyal to the king. As the fortunes of war ebbed and flowed, the town was garrisoned first by one side and then by the other. From 1643 a number of soldiers' burials are recorded in the registers, including one of a deserter who was 'hanged upon the Swan sign-post'. Various skirmishes took place in the neighbourhood. During all the troubled years of the war the ordinary people of Hampshire had to endure requisitioning and looting by troops of both sides, but after the formation of the New Model Army in 1645 under General Fairfax, a greater discipline was imposed: the register records the burial on May 10th of *a soldier, name unknown, hanged for murther when Sir Thomas Fairfax was throwe*. The unfortunate trooper had been sentenced to death the previous day at Ringwood for burglary and murder and Fairfax took the opportunity, as he marched his troops through Romsey, to carry out the sentence.[6]

In 1641 Parliament ordered the churchwardens of every parish to move the communion table from the east end, take away railings, crucifix and candles and level the chancel. Bishops, deans and chapters were all abolished and the Directory was substituted for the Prayer Book. Anyone using the Prayer Book was fined £5 for the first offence, £10 for the second and given three years' imprisonment for the third. Many clergymen were deprived of their livings for refusing to comply: some were executed. Their goods were confiscated and their families reduced to penury. When Sir William Waller's troops entered Winchester in 1642, the townspeople paid £1,000 to be saved from pillage, but the soldiers plundered the clergy houses in the close. They broke into the cathedral, rode up the nave, destroyed the altar, burnt the prayer books and scattered the bones of the Saxon kings and saints from the mortuary chests.

Soon it was Romsey's turn. On March 4th 1643, Waller's men marched on the town. They entered the abbey, pulling up the seats and destroying the organ. Then, according to a contemporary chronicler, *'a zealous brother of the ministry, dwelling not far off, got into the pulpit and for the space of two hours, in a furious zeal, applauded that religious act, encouraging them to go on as they had begun'.*[7] It is hard to imagine the state in which the church was left: an officer had to be paid for finding the Communion chalice which had been looted by the soldiers. It was during this raid that a cannonade of artillery pitted the north wall of the north transept. The marks are still visible but whether the shots were fired in warning, in target practice or from sheer devilment is not known.[8]

We can only guess at the feelings of the learned vicar at these unhappy events. He clearly had to keep a low profile or he would have lost his job, if not his head. At first, it seems, he could not bring himself to conform to the Act of Parliament which required him to use the new Directory in place of the Prayer Book. A baptism in 1646 was administered not by the vicar but by another cleric, Dr. Faithful; a scornful note by White in the register records that the father from the pulpit gave thanks for his wife's safe delivery in her absence *'which was all the churching she had'*. Eventually he decided that it was prudent to comply. He records on March 13th 1647, *'Jone Moses, dau. of Nicholas, the first child which I baptized according to the new directory enjoyned by the ordnance of the Lords and Commons assembled in Parliament.'* His distaste for the new law is evident from the wording of the entry. He was not ejected but died in 1648, saddened no doubt by all the changes he had seen in Church and state. He was succeeded by the 'intruder' vicar, John Warren, so-called because he had not been episcopally ordained and presumably led a free church form of service.

The Restoration

At the Restoration (1660), there was not only a return to the monarchy but a restoration of episcopacy and traditional ways of worship expressed in a new Book of Common Prayer. John Warren, with his brother Thomas, the vicar of nearby Houghton, were among some 2,000 clergy in England who were ejected from their livings for refusing to comply with the Act of Uniformity which demanded that the clergy should give their unfeigned assent to the restored Prayer Book.

A further challenge to conscience came with the Test Acts. These required that all who held civil or military office should take communion in the Church of England at least once a year. A certificate had to be produced to show that they had done so. An example of an 18th century communion certificate, signed by John Peverel the vicar, is in the glass case at the west end of the church. The Act was not repealed until the 19th century but was the cause of much hypocrisy while it was enforced.

William and Mary

In spite of such restrictions, there was a growing spirit of religious tolerance spreading in the country. After the ascent to the throne of William and Mary in 1689 an Act of Toleration was passed which allowed freedom of worship for non-conformists. One result of this was the burial of the much-respected ex-vicar of Houghton, Thomas Warren, in the abbey in 1693 in spite of his independent views. A fulsome tribute may be read on his gravestone on the floor of the south transept. The wording of the inscription and an explanation of the double date of death will be found in Appendix Seven.
Victorian to modern times

Changes in fashion and swings of doctrinal emphasis have caused several re-orderings of the chancel in more recent times. Victorian clergy, under Tractarian influence, revived medieval ceremonial and deliberately separated clergy from laity in an attempt to bring awe and reverence back into Eucharistic worship after the casual attitudes of the 18th century. The Rev. E.L.Berthon, vicar of Romsey between 1860 and 1892, was responsible for a great deal of restoration in the abbey — some of his achievements are listed below — but in Victorian style he divided the chancel from the nave by a screen and had stalls made in the chancel for a surpliced choir: an innovation which, in his own words, was fought tooth and nail.

In the present century the chancel has been opened up again and the introduction of modern forms of service with their emphasis on lay participation has brought the clergy once again closer to the people. There

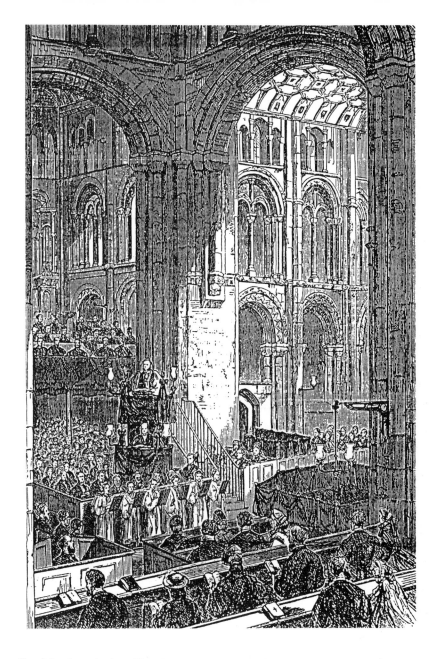

Church interior at the time of Lord Palmerston's death in 1865, before the galleries were removed.
Mourning drapes on Palmerston pew.

are likely to be further swings of fashion and strongly-held views can still cause controversy, but nowadays the Church has moved beyond the imposition of a set of beliefs through fines, persecution or excommunication.

II. CHANGES DUE TO PRACTICAL NECESSITY

Draughts and Dilapidation

A visitor to the abbey today would hardly recognize the interior as it looked a few centuries ago. A clergyman visiting the town in 1742 complained of over 40 windows stopped up with bricks. He added that church cleaning costs were infinitesimal and nothing at all spent on heating, although the services of the clerk were required occasionally to 'salt the fleas' in the square pews of the notables.[9]

The chancel archways had been filled with rubble to keep out draughts; in the south triforium of the nave they were blocked for the same reason and to avoid the expense of repairing the nave aisle roof. Galleries were built in the transepts and an organ loft blocked the western chancel arch. It was later moved westwards to the third bay of the nave. Charles Spence, writing his *Handbook to Romsey Abbey* in 1841, complained of the unsightly curtain which obstructed the view and was a monument of bad taste and a harbour for dust.[10] It had been hung behind the organ in 1833 in a further attempt to block out draughts and had presumably been gathering dust and cobwebs ever since.

Drawings of the period show a font at the west end of the nave, which was otherwise bare of furniture, but at the end of the 18th century we hear of baptisms taking place in the vestry because the church was so cold and damp.[11]

Another visitor of the 19th century wrote a letter of complaint to the editor of the *Gentleman's Magazine:*

> *You, of course, know Romsey Abbey but those of your readers who have not visited it, and yet are acquainted with its merits and interest by means of books, articles and prints would hardly believe the unworthy state in which it is kept. A ludicrous and yet offensive corporation pew, a closely-packed block of pews in*

West end and font. Note Early English arches; no vaulting in nave aisle

77

the nave, two ugly galleries in the transepts, a miserable but cumbrous pulpit overtopping a roomy reading-desk, a nondescript piece of carpentry called by courtesy an inner porch deform this noble building. The exterior is in a lamentable state of decay; the ground rises upwards of two feet against the walls; iron stack-pipes disfigure the apsidal chapel of the south transept, which has lost its conical roof; while a corresponding chapel on the north side is a receptacle for parish engines, ladders, and all kinds of rubbish. A long shed for ladders, some feet in height, has been built along the side of the choir; and neglect has left the southern portion of the yard a mass of tall weeds.[12]

The chancel ceiling

Chancel c.1800 showing part of compartmented ceiling

At one time a compartmented ceiling (of painted canvas) covered the chancel which helped to enclose the area and afford a little protection from the cold. The line of this ceiling is still visible on the stonework. It is described by the antiquarian, Dr. Latham, who says that the compartments were painted alternately with red roses and the Romsey portcullis, supported on each side with a red dragon. The ceiling (believed to have been of canvas) was curved and on the lower compartments saints and martyrs were depicted. It must have been quite handsome, but as the painting deteriorated, it was covered over with whitewash along with all the walls and piers and eventually it was removed.

'The chalk pit'

The earliest record we have of the whitewashing of the church is in the parish register for 1623: 'This year was begun the painting of our church'. Lime washing was common as a means of preserving the stonework. In the winter when outdoor workers, unable to find employment, applied to the parish for relief, they would be put to work by the overseer to renew the whitewash. Over the centuries there was such a build-up of the paint that all the zigzag decoration of the archways and the sculpture on the capitals became obliterated. They were only re-discovered by William Major, an energetic sexton with antiquarian interests in the last century, who described the interior as looking like a great chalk pit. The whitewash was cleaned off with great difficulty as part of the expensive restoration begun in the 1840s.

Schools held in the church

There are various references to schools, probably a free school and a grammar school, being held in different parts of the church building. Over the centuries the schoolboys no doubt contributed to the wear and tear.

From 1536 parish clergy were required to see that all children received basic reading lessons and religious instruction.[13] As this duty, if carried out at all, would normally fall on the parson, it was natural that the teaching should have taken place in the church.

At one time a school was held in the eastern apse of the north transept: it was later put to even more ignoble use as a fire station with a shed built up against it. There may also have been a school in the retrochoir. In 1712 a licence was applied for to build a school-room: this probably refers to the gallery which was built in the north-west corner of the church, creating class-rooms at two levels. A number of carved initials and dates may still be seen there at first-floor level. By 1826 Lord Palmerston was lending support to the building of a new school because the abbey school-room was overcrowded and the boys were causing damage in the churchyard by playing there before and after school.[14] That school catered for 100 boys and new premises were opened for them in 1836, but schooling of some kind was still continuing in the abbey. Mudie's *Hampshire* (1838) speaks of a part of the south aisle 'parted off and used for Sunday and other schools'.

Doorways everywhere!

In the unsuccessful struggle to defeat the cold and draughts in the church, different entrances were opened up but frequently blocked off again. There is a small Tudor door in the north transept wall which is now used only by the bell-ringers. It gives access to a spiral staircase which leads to an open gallery above the transept and thence to the ringing chamber. Originally it also gave access to the transept. About two feet to the west of it a larger door is dated 1739; this is also now blocked off, but it must originally have replaced an older door because its porch, created in the thickness of the wall and now used as a cleaning cupboard, has a number of initials and dates scratched on the walls which date between 1624 and 1648. A few feet east of these two doors there is a low window, now blocked; possibly it gave a slanting view through the wall to the transept altar so that people could watch when mass was celebrated. It has been suggested that it was a lepers' window or even that it gave access to an anchorite's cell, but there is no evidence for that.

From the 18th century the main entrance for the congregation was through a door at the easternmost end of the north wall (where there is now a cleaning cupboard below a window). Prior to that there was a door at the east end leading into what is nowadays St. Mary's chapel. The butt joint of this door is visible outside.

The new door made a more imposing entrance with steps leading down from some gates, but it still created draughts, so in 1825 two enormous doors were erected which extended across the whole width of the two chancel aisles and reached the archways above. They were popularly

80

North side of church c.1820 **Doors from left to right:**

a.   North door, at one time main entrance
b.   Large door dated 1723
c.   Tudor door leading to stairs to ringing chamber
d.   Present north entrance without a porch
e.   Small door leading to schoolroom

Note marks showing high pitch of earlier transept and nave roofs, and remains of precinct wall still standing at west end.

known as the 'Gates of Gaza'. They were opened on Sundays, but closed five minutes before the service began. After that, one could enter by a small door within the larger one, described as a 'cloth wicket'. The hope had been that these large doors would create a kind of vestibule out of the ambulatory and keep the worst of the cold out of the main body of the church. Draughts, however, still swirled round the interior, so these entrances were later demolished and a southern doorway opened up. With the building of separate school premises, the door in the north-west corner opening into the old school rooms was also blocked up.

The apple tree on the abbey roof

There are 18th century drawings and references to the apple tree which for more than a century grew on the roof above the retrochoir. The people of Romsey were proud of this curiosity, although it was further evidence of the neglected state of the church. It presumably germinated accidentally from a pip and flourished in the accumulation of dirt and pigeon droppings. It is said to have borne two kinds of fruits - red shanked and golden pippins - which were sold by the sexton as a curiosity for a penny a piece. The tale grew that the tree produced not two, but three and even seven varieties! As pennies had some value in those days, one suspects that when the tree's own crop ran out, the sexton supplemented the supply with varieties from his own garden. This may explain the strange phenomenon! The tree eventually died and was removed in 1824.

Restoration and Renewal

Fortunately two great Victorian vicars had the vision, means or influence to repair the fabric of the church, to sweep away the excrescences and restore its former beauty. The first was the Hon. Gerard Noel who was vicar in the decade up to 1840. The second was Edward Lyon Berthon, the incumbent for over 30 years from 1860. His re-ordering of the chancel has already been mentioned, but he was a man of wide interests and many talents as an inventor, astronomer and amateur artist (see below p.128), and he put his gifts to use in the restoration of the abbey.

There was opposition to some of the changes proposed and there were the usual problems of fund-raising, but gradually the hideous galleries were swept away, ugly box pews removed and the vista from west to east opened

SOUTH TRANSEPT &
CHOIR ROMSEY
ABBEY.

83

up. Cartloads of rubble were taken away as windows and archways were unblocked, and essential repairs were made to the roofs and stonework. Berthon was responsible for installing huge Gurney heating stoves (for which Lord Palmerston contributed £40). They at last produced some degree of warmth in the nave and meant that the entire area could be opened up for the congregation.

SOURCES ON DOCTRINAL CHANGES

Addleshaw & Etchells, *The Architectural Setting of Anglican Worship*
J.R.H.Moorman, *A History of the Church in England*, 3rd ed.1980

REFERENCES

1. J.E.Paul, Hampshire, *Recusants in time of Elizabeth I*, HFC vol.21, pt.II, 1959
2. Latham, vol.II, 68R
3. G.R.Balleine, *The Layman's History of the Church of England*
4. Luce, p.59
5. VCH vol.II, p.96
6. HFC, vol.XVI, pt.I
7. Luce, p.61
8. As late as 1969, it is recorded that a cannon ball was preserved in the vestry (*Romsey Magazine*, Nov.1969): it has since vanished.
9. Letter from Rev.Benjamin Newcome, quoted by Mrs Suckling, *Bye-gone Romsey*
10. C. Spence, *Handbook*, 1841 ed., p.123
11. *Archaeologia*, 1794, article on old font
12. *Gentleman's Magazine*, 1862, pt.II, pp.208-209
13. C.Hibbert, *The English, A Social History*, p.265
14. P. Genge & J. Spinney, *Romsey Schools*, p.34

CHAPTER EIGHT

POST-REFORMATION MONUMENTS AND MEMORIALS

(The list of memorials below is confined to those which have most historical or artistic interest.)

At the WEST END

The Font was given in 1912 by Canon Cooke Yarborough, the vicar, in memory of his only son. It may be noted that the church boasts three fonts, but none of any antiquity. The second font, in the north aisle, is a Victorian copy of a Gothic font. It is not often used but it marks the spot where the font of the medieval parish stood (see above p.28). The original font may have been the one which, much to the disgust of William Major, the sexton of the time, was broken up and its stone used when a doorway at the west end of the north aisle was being filled up in 1847. According to the sexton, the old font could easily have been restored with very little trouble or expense. There is also a third small font of no great age in the north choir aisle.

The Palmerston memorials

On the west wall three tablets commemorate members of the Palmerston family. The first Viscount Palmerston purchased Broadlands in 1736. The third viscount (the Prime Minister) died in 1865 and left the estate to his widow for life and then to her son by a previous marriage, William Cowper-Temple, who was later created Lord Mount Temple.

The tablet on the left commemorates Henry, the second viscount and father of the Prime Minister, who died in 1802, and his second wife Mary who died in 1805. The sculptor was John Flaxman, the designer of Wedgwood pottery. His style is very evident in the two genii holding a wreath in the Grecian pediment above the inscription.

This was apparently Flaxman's last work. A contemporary recorded:

The unexpected death of John Flaxman RA occasioned much regret at Romsey as the melancholy intelligence was received at the moment when his assistant was in the act of erecting a monument executed by him to the late Lord and Lady Palmerston, which is a most chaste and elegant specimen of the talents of the late sculptor...[1]

The central memorial is to Henry's first wife Frances, who died in childbirth in 1769. It was designed by Robert Adam and executed by Thomas Carter. It is a fine piece of simple ornamental carving with just a tiny figure in a roundel at the top. The inscription extols her virtues in the flowery style typical of the period.

The right-hand tablet commemorates Sir William Temple, the brother of the Prime Minister. The design on this plaque is a copy of the Flaxman tablet.

The Prime Minister, who was the third viscount, was of course buried in Westminster Abbey, but in his memory the west windows were filled with stained glass, since removed (see p.118). His surviving memorial in Romsey is the fine bronze statue by Matthew Noble on a plinth of polished pink granite which stands in the Market Place.

Sir William Petty (1623-1687)

One of the most distinguished figures of the 17th century, a contemporary and friend of Samuel Pepys, was born and buried in Romsey. His monument in Carrara marble, sculpted by Richard Westmacott, was erected by a descendant, Henry Marquis of Lansdowne, in 1858. Looking considerably handsomer than in a contemporary portrait (where he appears heavy-featured with hook nose and double chin), his head rests on an embroidered cushion and he holds a scroll with the seal of the Royal Society of which he was a founder member. The surrounding inscription describes him as a *true patriot and a sound philosopher who, by his powerful intellect, his scientific works and indefatigable industry, became a benefactor to his family and an ornament to his country*. In contrast, his grave slab on the floor of the south choir aisle says simply HERE LAYES SIR WILLIAM PETY.

This son of a Romsey clothier was born in Church Street in a handsome house later destroyed by fire. The site, between nos. 28-32, is marked by a commemorative plaque. Petty achieved fame in the very different fields of political economy, anatomy, natural science and mathematics, and as an inventor, writer, entrepreneur, cartographer and statistician.

The young William had acquired a basic grammar school education, but times were hard in Romsey and his father had debts, so at the age of 14 he went to sea. Being put ashore in France with a broken leg, he gained admission to the University of Caen and claimed that by the age of 15 he had mastered Latin, Greek and French, the whole body of arithmetic, practical geometry and astrology! He went on to other continental universities, later studying medicine at Oxford and becoming Professor of Anatomy. However, he had too much energy and organizing talent to settle for an academic life and within a few years we find him in Ireland, after the Cromwellian re-conquest, undertaking a great survey of the country as a basis for dividing up the forfeited land. He was a shrewd businessman and succeeded over this period in acquiring and developing great estates in Ireland for himself. This involved him in many lawsuits and made him enemies, one of whom challenged him to a duel. The near-sighted Petty suggested hatchet and axe in a dark cellar, upon which his opponent withdrew.

Petty had a fertile imagination as well as inexhaustible energy. At the age of 25 he had applied for a patent for an instrument for double writing (when there were no carbons, let alone photocopies). He also spent many years on the development of a double-bottomed ship, but the idea finally had to be abandoned. He would have liked a political career, but in that he was disappointed. Some of his ideas were far-sighted: he wanted unemployment assistance, a state medical service, compulsory land registry and a decimal coinage.[2]

Alice Taylor

In complete contrast with the distinguished William Petty, the other monument at the west end commemorates a child who would have been long forgotten if she had not been immortalized through her father's love. Alice was the two-year old daughter of a local doctor and gifted amateur sculptor (he exhibited a pieta in the 1851 Exhibition). The child died in 1843 from scarlet fever and her grieving father kept her memory alive with this life-size model of his daughter lying as if asleep.

The simple inscription: *Is it well with the child? It is well* is from II Kings, chap.4. A leaflet is available in the church with fuller details about Dr Taylor and his family.

In the SOUTH TRANSEPT

John and Grissell St. Barbe (d.1658)

This quaint monument is believed to be by Thomas Stanton but has been considerably restored. At the top are the St.Barbe arms (chequy argent and sable with the wivern crest). Beneath these are the two busts of John St.Barbe and Grissell, separated by their impaled arms. In the panel below is an epitaph, verse and curious anagram on their names:

> *An Epitaph upon John St.Barbe Esq. the sone of Henry St.Barbe Esq. and Grissell his wife, the daughter of John Pynsent Esq. He about the 42 yeare of his age and she the 22 yeare of her age, leaving fower sonns, Henry, John, Francis and Edward, slept in ye Lord.*
>
> *Earth's rich in Mines of pretious Dust*
> *Since in her Bowels rest these just*
> *Whom Nature Wedlock Grace did*
> *tie In one fast Chain of unity*
> *And faithfull ones*
> *Whose silent Bones*
> *Dead here do Rest yet left not Earth*
> *But brought fower Sonns to Perfect Birth Because such Righteous*
> *and theire Seed Shall flourish here and shall in Deed In Fame and State*
> *Tryumph o're Fate*
>
> *An Anagram upon theire names*
> *John* } *Sainte Barbe*
> *Grissel*
> *BE IN SHARES IN BLEST GLORIE*

St. Barbe monument in the South transept

89

(Sainte may have been spelt Seinte before restoration, which would make the anagram correct.)

At the base of the monument are the four sons in red gowns with white caps and collars, all but one holding a plant of life: this one was Henry who seems to have died before the monument was erected.

John St.Barbe inherited Broadlands (lately the home of Lord Mountbatten) through the marriage of his grandfather to Frances Fleming. Frances' own grandfather, William Fleming, had married Jane, who was the daughter of John Foster, the receiver and chaplain of the abbey, and Jane Wadham, the former nun (see p.61). The family history was thus linked with the last days of the nunnery.

The St.Barbes were an ancient family with an estate at Ashington in Somerset. John's father seems to have lived in retirement there in the civil war and to have taken no part in politics, but both his sons, along with many Hampshire landowners, fought on the parliament side. Francis, the elder son, died of wounds received at the first Battle of Newbury, leaving John as heir to Broadlands.

John had represented Southampton in the parliament of July 1654, but in 1658 he and his wife died within hours of each other of an illness described as the 'sweating sickness'. There had been violent outbreaks of an illness known by this name in the fifteenth and sixteenth centuries. The symptoms were described as 'grete stynking', fever and sometimes black spots. The coronation of King Henry VII was postponed until this strange pestilence had subsided.[3] Whether the 1658 contagion was the same or more akin to influenza is not clear, but apparently there was an outbreak of a virulent fever at this time.

Of the four unfortunate orphans, only John survived to full manhood. Sir John St.Barbe (a baronetcy had been bought for him as a boy: a common practice for gentlemen of wealth) engaged in various forms of public service. Among his benefactions, he left a bequest to the charity school in Romsey to support ten poor boys and the master. After his death, Broadlands passed to a relative who sold it to Lord Palmerston.

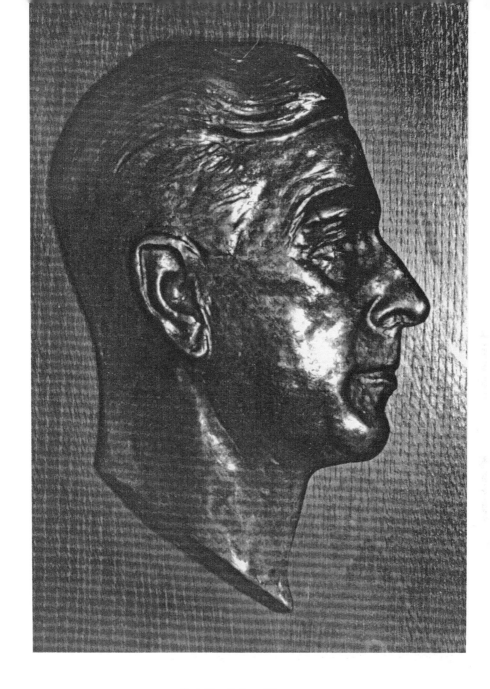

Earl Mountbatten of Burma

Lord Mountbatten

At the foot of the St.Barbe monument is buried Admiral of the Fleet, Earl Mountbatten of Burma. The simple slate tombstone is on the site which he himself had chosen. Broadlands was his home, inherited by his wife, Edwina, and now occupied by his grandson, Lord Romsey.

Lord Mountbatten was a great-grandson of Queen Victoria. His tragic assassination in 1979 ended a long life of public service. At the west end of the church hang his flags: on the north side is his personal flag as Supreme Allied Commander of South-East Asia in Singapore 1945, while the one to the south was flown in Delhi in 1947 when he was last Viceroy of India. The bronze heads of Lord and Lady Louis on the Broadlands pew in the chancel were made in Malta at the time of Lady Louis' death in 1960. As she was buried at sea, this is her only memorial. Lord Louis' own head was not put on until after his death but portrays him as he was twenty years earlier.

John Kent

This memorial to John Kent who died in 1692 is one of the finest in the church. Latham describes it as follows:

> The monument is of white marble having a large swelling tablet in the middle on which is the inscription. The monument has on each side a Corinthian column supporting a pediment above, dividing in the middle to have place to a small urn, the cover and base of which is ornamented with flutings and the head with an ornament of leaves; the bottom of each pillar rests first on a curved bracket and (is) ultimately supported by a death's head under each. Between the brackets under the inscription is a second tablet ornamented with palm branches and other devices, and this last finishes beneath with a cherub with expanded wings.[4]

John Kent was a poor boy of the town. Assisted by a kind benefactress he went to London and made good as a 'silk thrower'. He was twice mayor of Romsey and later became high sheriff of the county. He founded almshouses in the town which still bear his name and made other generous bequests to its inhabitants.

The term 'silk-thrower' needs explanation. The silkworm cocoons are gently baked in an oven and then, after being soaked in warm water, the silk is 'reeled' by taking five or six threads and winding them together into a long thread. This is called raw silk. It is then twisted with several other threads to make the yarn. This is the process called throwing.[5]

The Latin inscription with its translation will be found in Appendix Eight.

John Storke

Around the corner in the choir aisle there is another large marble memorial to John Storke and other members of his family. He died in 1711 and was evidently a merchant. There is a ship at the top of each corner and originally there was a large ship in full sail on top of the central coat of arms (which contains the arms of Storke and Williams impaled[6]). This ship had to be removed to make way for the panel of medieval glass inserted in the window above. This monument is flamboyant but less artistic than the Kent memorial: the tablet is flat and the lettering inferior.

Thomas Warren

On the floor of the same transept there may be found a memorial inscription to Thomas, the brother of John Warren, the vicar described as intruder. Like John, Thomas was puritan by conviction and unable to subscribe to Church of England doctrine after the Restoration. He lost his living at Houghton and for some years could only minister privately to those of his persuasion. After 1672 he and other Independents were permitted to register as Presbyterians and to his small flock the present United Reformed Church in Romsey owes its origin.

The fact that he was buried in the abbey in spite of his nonconformist views is testimony to his reputation for powerful preaching and personal piety. The wording of the inscription is striking:

> *Here lyeth ye body of Thos Warren*
> *a learned pious and faithfull Minister of Christ*
> *a solid and nervous assertor of*
> *discriminating grace and freed will*
> *who died Jan ye 27 1693/4 aged 77*

(The word 'nervous' meant 'vigorous' in those days. For an explanation of the alternative years of death, see Appendix Seven.)

In the RETRO-CHOIR

Maud Ashley

This monument in white marble has been described as being in the French Salon style of the 18th century.

Maud was the wife of Wilfrid Ashley (Lord Mount Temple of Lee). She died of tuberculosis in 1913 at the early age of 30, leaving two young daughters: Edwina, who became Countess Mountbatten of Burma, and Mary, who became Lady Delamere.

Richardson and Gill were the architects responsible for the general design and Emil Fuchs was the sculptor. Fuchs was eminently suited to undertake this commission. He was an Austrian-born scuptor, painter and medallist who had settled in England. He had executed portrait medals of Queen Victoria, Edward VII and other distinguished people and he had won a gold medal in Munich for a group in marble entitled 'Mother's Love'. The Maud Ashley composition reflects the same theme of motherhood: she is seated on some steps, embracing the naked figures of her two daughters who are partially covered by her cloak. Maud's head also appears in relief on a pillar behind.

Above the NORTH DOOR

Hatchment of Lord Montagu Bertie

This diamond-shaped panel containing a coat of arms is an example of a funeral hatchment which sets forth the rank and circumstances of a deceased person. It was hung on his house during the period of mourning and then placed in the church. Hatchments first appeared in England in the early 17th century, but were commonest in the late 18th and early 19th centuries. They were the last display of heraldry and were usually executed by the coach builders who would already have painted the deceased's coat of arms on the side of his coach.

'Hatchment' is a distortion of the word 'achievement' as coats of arms were intended to illustrate a person's family and background. In the case of a married man, his arms were shown impaled with those of his wife. The background of his own arms was painted black in mourning. The central feature of a hatchment is a shield. The helm above shows the man's rank. Other features are supporters (i.e. figures flanking the shield and supporting it), drapes which swirl from the helm and the family motto.

Captain Lord Montagu Bertie RN (the name is pronounced 'Barty'), who is commemorated in this hatchment, was the third son of Robert, first Duke of Ancaster. His arms are described below. He married Anne, daughter of William Piers, MP for Wells, and died in 1753. His wife's arms are of a pelican with a chick pecking her breast. This motif is commonly known as the 'pelican in piety'. (There was an archbishop of York called Piers in the reign of Queen Elizabeth I who bore these arms.)

Captain Bertie lived at Lee Manor on the Broadlands estate, a house later demolished by Lord Palmerston. His burial is not recorded in the parish register, but in the Poor Rate book for Romsey Extra he was assessed in 1752 for 1s.10d. After that, Lady Montagu Bertie's name appears until 1761 when it vanishes.

Heraldic description
Motto: Loyalty me oblige
Arms: Argent, three battering rams proper, headed azure
Crest : A saracen's head, couped at the shoulders proper, crowned or
Supporters: Dexter, a pilgrim or friar, vested in russet, with his crutch or and rosary or
Sinister, a savage man, wreathed about the temples and waist with ivy proper
(Strictly speaking, Captain Bertie was not entitled to show supporters)

Other Memorials

Other memorials are to persons now unknown but still of interest because they bring history to life as well as illustrating some of the triumphs and tragedies of the human condition. For example, Ann Moody (west wall of south transept) reminds us of the tragically high mortality from childbirth. She died in 1780 aged 19 with her infant son: *'Look on this monument, ye gay and careless... and boast no more of tomorrow'*. Of similar date is 'Honest Gaspar' (retrochoir) a Greek, according to the register. He served his family for 60 years and his grateful master commends him to the rising generation in his line of life to imitate his worthy example. More recently, there is a monument (north aisle) to a young engineer who went down with the Titanic on its fateful maiden voyage in 1913.

For artistic merit, mention should be made of the cartouche tablet decorated with angels' and deaths' heads in the retrochoir. It commemorates a vicar, William Mayo, who died in 1727 and his wife Elizabeth, daughter of George Gollop, owner of the local manor of Stanbridge Earls.

REFERENCES

1.   Latham, vol.II, 175v.
2.   Sources on Petty:
a. P.G.Dale, *Sir W.P. of Romsey*
b. E.Strauss, *Sir William Petty, Portrait of a Genius*
c. Latham, vol.III
3.   *The Times*, 26 July 1825; symptoms described in Hibbert, *The English, A Social History* p.162
4.   Latham, vol.II,80V
5.   I am indebted to article by Tony Vanderplank in *Romsey Magazine*, November 1980 for this information.
6.   Latham, vol.II, 79R

CHAPTER NINE

'Make a joyful noise to God'

1. ROMSEY ORGANS

The earliest organs were simple instruments which could be played by one hand while the other hand worked the bellows. They seem to have originated in the east and had found their way to England by Saxon times. The first church organs to be mentioned were installed by the sixth century, but are said to have been raucous and unwieldy. Malmesbury Abbey appears to have had an organ in the time of King Edgar[1]. It was only in the thirteenth century that the mechanism of organs was improved and their tone softened. However, it is likely that the nuns of Romsey sang unaccompanied. Many medieval instruments are only known to us through their appearance in sculptures. The only one connected with the abbey is to be found on a corbel of a fiddler at the south side of the chancel. His instrument is a rebec. He probably played it more on civil than on religious occasions.

Corbel of fiddler

Richard Wale's gift

The earliest mention we have of an organ in the abbey is in 1637 at the christening of Anne Appleford, the town clerk's daughter. The register records:

> Some of the quire of Winton came over and sang some sacred anthems, our organs going with them

This became garbled in the memory of a late vicar, Canon Norris, who thought he had read somewhere that at that date our choir had gone to Winchester to sing, taking our organ with them.[2] In such a way are myths created!

97

In the parish register two years later, we discover the name of the donor of this organ:

Richard Wale, ye elder, buried, giver of a new organ to the church.

Richard Wale's organ may not have survived very long, as in the civil war which broke out shortly afterwards we learn that in 1643 parliamentary troops under the command of Sir William Waller marched on Romsey and defaced the abbey church 'pulling up the seats and destroying the organ'.[3]

For the next century we have no information as to music in the abbey. Under the Commonwealth there was presumably almost none. After the Restoration, if the organ had been destroyed, there may have been a band of musicians to lead the singing.

The Coster Organ

In 1782 we hear of a new organ, provided by voluntary subscription, which was built by Coster of Salisbury. To celebrate its installation and to contribute, no doubt, to the organ fund about 700 people were present at a grand oratorio. It appears to have been a great social occasion with all the local gentry turning up in their carriages for the recital. The oratorio was advertised in the Winchester and Salisbury papers which stated that many capital performers had been engaged for it.[4]

The vestry minute book for that year refers to a fund set up to support the organist who had been appointed together with a bellows blower.
The fame of the oratorio reached the ears of the diocesan authorities who enquired why no licence to install an organ had been applied for. The churchwarden protested that a licence was not necessary as there had previously been an organ in the church. He was apparently over-ruled, as a petition was then submitted to grant a faculty for an organ already purchased. It stated:

> *That there is a gallery already erected under the arch which separates the body* (i.e. the nave, not then used for seating) *from the church of Romsey aforesaid, in which gallery they have placed the said organ ... without interfering with, infringing upon, injuring or disturbing any of the parishioners or inhabitants of the said parish ... and will*

1838 View of nave from chancel, showing Coster organ and huge curtain behind it

do no injury to walls or fabric, but is an ornament and will assist in worship. (signed) John Woodburn, vicar.[5]

The faculty was granted, but it was not long before the organ began to give trouble. In 1796 an estimate for repair was obtained from a London firm, but it was higher than the cost of the original organ and the churchwardens in true laissez-faire spirit resolved to leave the organ in its present state but not to play it! For a while the psalms were in part accompanied by wind instruments. However, on Easter Day Mr Endle, the organist, made another attempt to coax some music out of it and then made an agreement with a carpenter to effect some repairs. Some new bellows were made at a cost of £15. These worked so well that it was determined to put in some work on the pipes as well. It is not surprising that comments were often heard that the organ was not as good as the church deserved.

In 1824, to allow for extra seating for the expanding population, the organ and gallery were moved further west to the third bay of the nave. Until that time, the congregation had been seated under the tower and in galleries across the transepts.

Over the next fifteen years the need for a new organ was frequently mooted but lack of funds and the pressing need for other repairs led to postponement of the project. In the first edition of Charles Spence's *Handbook*[6], he described the Coster organ as:

> *an instrument whose asthmatic pipes do their best to convince us of the almost incredible fact of its ever having been a healthy organ.*

After 1855, in later editions, he could report that the gallery which had marred the fine effect of the nave had been swept away, together with the condemned organ.

A second musical hiatus

There was a period of about three years when the abbey had no organ. The few members of the choir sat at the far west end and, according to local recollections, Mrs Tylee, a member of a well-known local family, used to give the key-notes with pitch pipes.

The Walker Organ

Faced with a large expenditure, our Victorian forefathers behaved exactly as we would today and set up a fund-raising committee: it included all the town's most prominent citizens.[7] The adviser to the committee was the Rev. Sir Frederick Ouseley, Professor of Music at Oxford. Several offers of second-hand instruments were discussed, but Ouseley strongly recommended the purchase of a purpose-built organ from the firm of J.W.Walker of London. Ouseley himself offered to add an improvement to the organ worth at least £30, once the fund reached the figure of £560. The siting of the organ caused some dispute: many people favoured a position at the west end, but this was objected to by Lord Palmerston as it would have obscured a family memorial. It was finally agreed that the organ and choir should be sited in the gallery which stood across the north transept. The new organ was accordingly installed there and dedicated at a service in November 1858 in the presence of Lord and Lady Palmerston. The final cost had amounted to £711 5s. 0d. There was still some deficit on the fund and no money available to supply a suitable case.

Ouseley wrote to the vicar, the Rev. C. Avery Moore, after the service to congratulate him on the new instrument. Ouseley himself had contributed a mixture stop in swell. He thought that the instrument produced admirable balance and mellowness and only regretted the lack of additional power for it, while admitting that it would be an expense beyond the resources of a town like Romsey to provide.

Removal to chancel

The Walker organ remained in the north transept for thirty years, but in 1882, the Rev. E.L.Berthon, the energetic and ingenious Victorian restorer, proposed ridding the church of its last unsightly galleries and the removal of the organ to its present position on the north side of the chancel. The vicar, anxious to be rid of the gallery, pointed out that the timber from it could be used to prepare the triforium gallery in the chancel to take the organ parts. Ouseley had been strongly in favour of providing the organ with a 32 ft. stop. It was therefore agreed to wait until funds were available for the new stop before moving and remodelling it. This time the fund-raising seems to have taken six years, but eventually donations made to mark the Queen's jubilee in 1887 allowed for the removal to be carried out in the following

Walker organ on the north side of the chancel

year. It was undertaken by the makers, Messrs Walker and Sons. Among the improvements carried out at the same time the swell and pedals were connected with a new patent tubular pneumatic action. This made all the difference to the touch which previously had been so heavy that the playing of a voluntary was described as a weariness of the flesh to the hapless performer.

Those with an interest in organs may like to know that the Romsey organ boasts about 2250 pipes of varying sizes, ranging from the small ones, about the size of a slim pencil, to the monster wooden 32 ft. pitch pipe which measures about two feet across.[8] This pipe is one of a number of diminishing pitch which are laid on their sides in the organ loft. The larger ones could be cleaned by the organ apprentice, working inside the pipes with a brush and pan. Those whose interest lies more in comparing the value of money at different dates may be interested to know that the work carried out in 1888 amounted to over £1,000 and that the organist's salary was raised from £30 to £40 p.a.

Later maintenance

Various problems required attention in the years immediately following the move and a somewhat acrimonious correspondence passed between the churchwardens and the firm, but eventually all parties were satisfied. After that no major repairs were needed for nearly a century. A full account of all the work that has been carried out on the organ over the years and technical details of the major expenditure now required to restore this historic instrument will be found in Appendix Nine.

Stairs to the ringing chamber

2. SUMMONED BY BELLS

From medieval times the people of Romsey have been summoned to worship by bells. We first have mention of them in a mandate from Pope Calixtus III in 1457, when he commanded that more or larger bells should be installed at the abbey as the existing ones could not be heard throughout the parish.[9] This conjures up a pleasant sense of continuity with the bell-ringers of today, but, as will be seen below, we are soon faced with some unanswerable questions.

The Old Belfry

It is known that there was a separate belfry which stood to the north-east of the parish church. (In 1900 a rent of £2 p.a. was still being paid to the church for an old cottage erected on the belfry ground.) By 1554 concern was being expressed about the safety of its structure, but what bells were being rung there? It is recorded that at the dissolution the six abbey bells were sold on behalf of the Court of Augmentations to John White, a citizen of London, along with 25 other bells from former monastic houses in the area.[10] Which bells were they?

Could there have been a reprieve for which the record is lost, because the bells were required to summon the people of Romsey to what was now their parish church? Clearly the parish was not left completely without bells because in 1558 Sir Francis Fleming left 20s. in his will 'towards hanging the bells in the tower'. Simon Clerke had left 13s. 4d. in the previous year for the same purpose, and in November 1558 John Judson left to the repairing of the parish bells 18s. *out of the cash for a goulden ring which Wm Blowes doth owe me.* [11]

The wills refer to the hanging or repair of the bells and not their purchase: the natural sense of these legacies is that some bells existed in an unsafe belfry and that funds were needed to re-hang them in the tower of the abbey where they are today.

Hiatus between 1558 and 1624

Why did sixty-six years elapse between these bequests and the hanging of the bells in the tower recorded in 1624? The money may have been

Abbey bells, cast 1791

the bells in the tower recorded in 1624? The money may have been insufficient, but this would have created something of a record in the history of parish fund-raising. Possibly it was decided that some repairs could be made to the belfry which prolonged its life for another half century. We cannot tell, but eventually the move was made.

The bells re-hung in the tower

The parish register for 1624 contains this record:[12]

> *This year were the bells hung up in the tower and the work finished in the month of November, a little before Christmas, and in the following January was the old belfry taken down.*

Until that date the tower had been open to the roof, but in 1624 a ceiling was inserted above the crossing in order to form a ringing chamber overhead, and the bells were placed in a wooden structure on the flat roof. This fine ceiling in Jacobean style is still to be seen today, but in the middle of the last century it was raised about 12 feet in order to reveal the very beautiful Norman arcading round the gallery.

We return to the problem of the bells. There could not have been two lots of bells, one for the parish and one for the nunnery, although there may have been a single bell in its own bell-tower within the enclosure to summon the sisters to their offices.

When the old bells were melted down in 1791, it was found that one dated from 1603, before the re-hanging in the tower, and another, undated, was of such antiquity that it was believed to have belonged to the nunnery. The others had been re-cast at different dates after 1624. They bore brief inscriptions or rhymes, as well as their dates. That on the fifth bell, dated 1630, read:

> *If with my fellows I agree*
> *Then listen to my harmony.*[13]

If the peal of six bells really was sold at the dissolution, possibly the old abbey bell was preserved and hung in the belfry with others, as acquired, until a new peal of six had been formed, but this is only conjecture.

107

These six bells were all large and, when moved to the tower, only five would fit in the wooden structure; the sixth had separate housing. Their great weight and the general lack of funds for maintenance caused problems in the post-Reformation period. Tragedy struck in 1638, when a burial is recorded:

May 11, John Adderley, killed in the tower by the fall of the great bell

There was either another fall later or else another long period of parish inaction. It was not until 1702 that an order was given to Clement Tozier of Salisbury to re-hang the Great Bell:

(He) shall hang up the Great Bell, being now in the tower in the same place where the same bell did lately hang, and take such care in hanging up and fixing, that it beare the same sound as it had before its fall (unless the same be crackt with that fall).

The new ring of bells

Whatever obscurities remain with regard to the old bells, their history came to an end in 1791, when they were sold for scrap to the Whitechapel Foundry of Thomas Mears and replaced by a new ring of eight. The scrap value of the old bells was £360 10s. 6d. to offset against the cost of £673 14s. 10d. for the new peal. Bell-ringers came from London to celebrate the opening.

On the first centenary of the new peal, in July 1891, the bells were rung at 5.30 am (!) and at intervals throughout the day until 9.0 pm. On the bi-centenary in 1991 the celebrations began less early but were no less joyful. The occasion was marked by the publication of a booklet on Romsey Abbey bells by Brian J.Woodruffe, an ex-captain of the ringers, which is available in the abbey. It recounts all the work carried out on the bells since 1791 and some of the changes which have been rung on them. The main overhaul was in 1932 when the bells were returned to the foundry to be repaired, quarter-turned and fitted with modern ball-bearings.

Curfew, fire alarms and the Death Knell

The curfew was rung during the winter months as a fire precaution. It was strictly enforced by William the Conqueror who ordered that fires and

108

lights everywhere should be put out when the bell was rung at 8 o'clock and not lit until it rang again at 4.0 am. Wealthy families owned a couvre-feu (the origin of the word 'curfew'), a metal or clay utensil similar to a shield in shape, with which they smothered the flames, but ordinary people would have damped them down with the cold ash from the back of the hearth and revived the embers the following morning. The curfew bell continued to be rung in Romsey up to the start of the Second World War.

Fire bells: The treble and second bells were rung from the crossing floor to alert the fire service.

For a long time the fire equipment was kept in the apse of the north transept. It consisted of little more than a hand-truck with stand-pipe and hoses for local use, although there was a horse-drawn truck with manual pumps for outlying districts.

The Death Knell: The tolling of this bell also continued in Romsey up to the beginning of World War II. It tolled three times three for a man, three times two for a woman and three times one for a child and then rang once for each year of their age. The name of the deceased was then posted on the church door.

The death knell had its origin in an even older custom known as the 'passing bell' which was rung, day or night, when a person was seen to be at death's door in order that all who heard it might offer prayers for the soul which was then leaving the body. It is referred to in a poem by the Elizabethan poet, George Gascoigne:

> *Alas, loe now I heare the passing bell,*
> *Which care appoynteth carefully to knowle,*
> *And in my brest I feele my heart now swell*
> *To breake the stringes which joynd it to my soule.*

After the Reformation, prayers for departed souls were forbidden and the passing bell became the death knell.

REFERENCES

1. Latham, vol.iv,p.33
2. *Romsey Advertiser*, July 1975
3. Luce, p.61
4. Suckling, *Byegone Romsey Infra*, XXVI
5. R.O. Faculties, 12 Dec.1782
6. Spence, Handbook, 1841 ed., p.121
7. The names of Messrs Jenvey, Perry, Linzee, Footner and Tylee are still familiar in the town
8. See Appendix Nine, for technical details of the organ
9. Coldicott, p.50
10. Coldicott, p.151
11. Liveing, p.271
12. H.F.C. vol.xvi, pt.I,1944
13. Latham, vol.v, p.51

The bell chamber

CHAPTER TEN

STAINED GLASS WINDOWS

Introduction

The technique of making translucent coloured glass and holding the pieces together with lead strips was established in Europe by the twelfth century. The glowing colours were made by adding various metallic oxides, such as cobalt, copper and iron, to the melted glass. A thin layer of this so-called pot-metal was applied to a sheet of plain glass to give a translucent effect.

When the Decorated style of architecture was introduced early in the fourteenth century, windows became far larger and the areas of glass between the vertical stone mullions became longer and narrower. Glass designers were faced with a problem of how to fill these tall narrow spaces and they solved it by placing elaborate architectural canopies above the figures. In all the larger windows in the abbey, Victorian designers have followed the same technique.

From 1530 onwards enamel painting on glass became increasingly common. It was easier and cheaper to produce than pot-metal and the designers could be more realistic. Enamel painting was used on virtually all glass made in the seventeenth and early eighteenth centuries. After that, the art of producing pot-metal glass was rediscovered and gradually artists learnt to combine the glowing colours of the past with their own freer and more flowing styles.

The Whitechapel firm of glaziers, James Powell & Son, which was founded in 1834 and only closed in 1973, was responsible for most of the good-quality Victorian glass in the abbey. The abbey is fortunate to have examples, albeit in small windows, of the work of two outstanding designers: Henry Holiday in the nineteenth century (north choir aisle) and Hugh Easton in the twentieth (south nave aisle). There is also some good work from the firm of Charles Kempe (see below).

Stained glass windows may be looked at for their artistic merit or for the historical interest of the personalities whom they commemorate, but from

Sketch of window from Rouen. Romsey panel is bottom right

Key to sketch (reading left to right and top to bottom)
(1 - 3) Creation and Garden of Eden   (4) Man's expulsion from garden
(5 - 6) Man tempted by sin (7 - 10) Life of Christ   (11) Ostentatious almsgiver
(12) Salvation

the time that they were first introduced into churches they have been intended to teach and inspire through their representations of the saints and Biblical themes.

Medieval glass

No stained glass from the nunnery has survived in the church, but there is one very fine panel of medieval glass in the south choir aisle[1]. It was given to the abbey in 1975 by Mrs Neill of Lee Park Farm in memory of her husband, Captain Charles Neill RAFVR, 1919-1970.

The glass is sixteenth century and was originally one of twelve panels from a window in the church of St.Nicolas in Rouen. The church was consecrated in 1533, closed in 1791 and demolished in 1840. The glass in it was dated 1540-1600 and was designed and made locally; indeed the church was popularly known as 'St.Nicolas des Painteurs'. The French Revolution and the Napoleonic Wars led to the secularisation of many churches and ecclesiastical authorities were only too willing to sell windows. The peace of Amiens in 1802 provided a good opportunity for Englishmen to travel on the continent. John Hampp, a Norwich textile merchant, and another man who was an antiquarian went round France, Germany and the Low Countries buying up stained glass. The account book kept by Hampp, still preserved in Cambridge, shows that in April 1903 he paid for some glass from Rouen. Mr Dennis King, who acquired the glass for Mrs Neill from a vendor near King's Lynn, believed that it had never left Norfolk from the time that Hampp brought it to England. A description of the glass was compiled in 1716-1722 by a French priest, Jean Barc, who sketched and described the panels.

It will be seen that the Romsey panel is the last scene in the bottom right-hand corner. The whole window is an allegory on the pilgrimage of the human soul. Man ('l'homme' in the inscription on the central figure on our panel) is seen with his pilgrim's staff in five of the panels (nos. 5, 6, 9, 11 and 12). After the creation of the world and the expulsion of Adam and Eve from the Garden of Eden (no.4), Man sets out in search of salvation which the Incarnation of Christ, prepared by the Annunciation (no.8) will bring him. There are several quaint details. For example, in nos.4-6 the devil appears carrying a flag with skull and crossbones on it. In nos.5 and 6 he is riding on a creature with seven heads to represent the seven deadly sins. No.7,

113

which is not mentioned by Jean Barc, shows a delightful little dog in front of what are surely the three Magi. Nos.8 and 9 on the Annunciation and the Preaching of Christ are the only other panels to have survived; both are in the Victoria and Albert's collection.

In both nos.11 and 12 are to be seen the ostentatious and the secret almsgivers contrasted in St.Matthew,vi,2-4. In no.11 the ostentatious almsgiver has a lackey in the top right corner who, according to Jean Barc, is blowing a trumpet. No.12 - our panel - has however a much deeper significance. Jean Barc gives it the title of 'Salvation' and it shows an angel coming down from heaven to receive the human soul at the end of his pilgrimage, saved by love (Charité) and prayer (Oraison - the third and least easily deciphered inscription). If you look at the window, you will see that Man is taking off for heaven - his feet no longer bear his weight - and he is clasping the secret almsgiver's left hand with his right hand, which is with some dexterity also carrying the pilgrim's staff. Behind the Man is the ostentatious almsgiver in a maroon gown, who looks extremely disgruntled at his rejection and has taken one or two gold coins out of the purse he was giving as alms to show how valuable the contents were.

Detail of Man rising heavenwards

A modern feature of the window is the crest of No.49 Squadron Bomber Command in which Captain Neill served while flying over Germany and occupied Europe during World War Two.

Victorian-Edwardian Glass

Kempe windows

There are three windows designed in the studios of the eminent Victorian stained glass artist, Charles Eamer Kempe. Kempe was prevented by a slight stammer from being ordained and decided to devote his life to the making of stained glass. His work has been described as prolific and sometimes monotonous — his firm produced over 4,000 windows in the space of sixty years — but it always shows competence and good taste.

In the east window of the north choir aisle the archangel Michael is overpowering the devil, represented by a dragon. The green peacock feathers are a favourite motif of Kempe's and sometimes replace his hallmark of a wheatsheaf. Around the figure are scattered monograms of the Virgin Mary. This window is dated 1897 and is in memory of Mrs G. B. Footner. The east and south windows of the south choir aisles depict the Epiphany and the child Jesus in the temple. These two windows were given in memory of the Hon. Evelyn Ashley (grandfather of Lady Louis Mountbatten) who died in 1907. Kempe died in the same year and was succeeded as chairman of his company by Walter Tower who adopted the hallmark of a tower superimposed on a wheatsheaf in order to underline the continuation of the master's tradition. Both symbols are to be found on these windows.

James Powell & Son Windows

(1) IN THE CHANCEL

The large east windows are in memory of Lord Mount Temple who died in 1888. He had inherited Broadlands from his step-father, Lord Palmerston. The inscription relates:

> *He served his country in Parliament for 53 years and his God through his life, being good to men and walking blamelessly before the Lord.*

115

The two windows form a single composition on the theme,

> *To the One who sits on the throne and to the Lamb be blessing and*
> *honour and glory and might.*
> (Canticle, *'A Song of the Redeemed'*)

The Mount Temple title inspired the left-hand scene from the verses,

> *Therefore are they before the throne of God and serve him day and*
> *night in his temple* (Rev.7,15), and *Ye are the temple of the living God*
> (II Cor.6,16);

while the right-hand depicts the Lamb from Rev.7,17:

> *The lamb shall lead them into living fountains of waters.*

Although the designer of this window is named as Charles Hardgrave, there is a noted added in the firm's order book[2], 'new cartoons by Sharp'. The explanation is probably that the faces of the worshippers are said to represent Mount Temple's friends in social and religious fields.   It is possible therefore that Sharp was the artist who drew in their faces in place of the stock features designed by Hardgrave.

(2) IN THE SOUTH TRANSEPT

The two central windows are in memory of the Hon. Ralph Heneage Dutton (d.1893) who lived at Timsbury Manor. They depict Christ walking with the disciples to Emmaus and making himself known in the breaking of bread. This time it is the face of the person commemorated which is given to the right-hand disciple in each of the windows.

The bottom windows are in memory of Georgiana Tollemache, Baroness Mount Temple, who died in 1901, and illustrated the miraculous draught of fishes and the commission to Peter: *Feed my lambs.*

(3) IN THE NORTH TRANSEPT

The Annunciation scene on the left is in memory of Almaric Rumsey of Lincoln's Inn, professor of Indian jurisprudence, who died in 1899. The

116

mosaic in the space above contains two coats of arms with vine scroll ornament in gold on a blue ground.

The right-hand window commemorates the Rev. E L Berthon whose long incumbency lasted from 1860 to 1892 (see p.128). The window depicts the Holy Family at Nazareth with Berthon's portrait and symbols of his varied interests as boat-builder, astronomer and inventor.

(4) IN THE NORTH CHANCEL AISLE

The window is in memory of Sybella Ashley, wife of the Hon. Evelyn Ashley, who died in the 1886 at the age of 40 after a long illness. It depicts the pool of Bethesda and bears the legend, *Jesus Christ maketh thee whole*. The designer of the exquisite small window was Henry Holiday, a first-rate artist, whose work has been described as 'earthy and colourful'[3].

Clayton & Bell

This was another well-known firm of Victorian glaziers which produced some high quality glass, but Romsey never benefited from their best work. Their two windows in the two small chapels in the retrochoir, depicting the Nativity and the Crucifixion, are undistinguished. The glass which they designed for the three lancet windows at the west end of the nave, which was paid for by public subscription in memory of Lord Palmerston, was described by the vicar of the time as 'the worst I have ever seen by Messrs Clayton & Bell'[4]. It was a period when the firm was producing too much fussy work with heavy colours. The windows must have darkened the church and many people were relieved when storm damage in 1961 necessitated the removal of the glass. The inscription recording the installation remains on the west wall and must cause some surprise to visitors who are unaware of the history. If they look up now, they will find only modern tinted glass in the windows.

Modern Glass

(1) NAVE AISLE near South Door

Hugh Easton, the designer of the small Annunciation scene, has been described as one of the outstanding artists of the twentieth century who have continued the tradition of representational painting[5]. He tends to use plenty of white glass to let in more light and combines bold, clear colours with great delicacy of design. His signature is in the compass points in the bottom right-hand corner. He designed the windows for the RAF memorial chapel in Westminster Abbey, where the same style and colours are to be seen on a larger scale.

(2) NORTH TRANSEPT (West Window)

Francis Skeat of St. Albans, another leading stained glass window designer of this century, was responsible for the window in memory of Canon William Henry Birch Corban who was a popular vicar of Romsey from 1925 to 1951. Around a central figure of St. Swithun carrying the arms of the see of Winchester, a series of heraldic shields mark Corban's life and career[6].

REFERENCES

1. Information originally obtained from Mr. Michael Archer, Victoria & Albert Museum, Captain Neill's window and Mr. Dennis King
2. Archive of Art & Design, AAD 1/9, 1977; 89/139(4367)
3. Painton Cowen, *A Guide to Stained Glass in Britain*
4. Berthon, p.161
5. Michael Archer, *Stained Glass* p.30 (Pitkin Pictorials)
6. Significance of shields, anti-clockwise from top:
    (a) three ravens for Corban (*corbus* = raven)
    (b) See of Gibraltar, where he was born in 1878, son of an army surgeon
    (c) City of Hereford, where he attended the cathedral school
    (d) Five chevrons azure: families of Avering or Evering (connection not known)
    (e) University of Cambridge
    (f) Clare College
    (g) Borough of Eastleigh, where he served his title
    (h) Diocese of Portsmouth, where he was vicar of St. Stephen's 1914-1925
    (i) Borough of Romsey

CHAPTER ELEVEN

GLIMPSES AND PORTRAITS

Bringing the Abbey to life

All great buildings and churches in particular, however beautiful, are lifeless without the human interest of the men who built them, the people who have worshipped in them and the moments of history to which they have formed the backdrop. In the course of the preceding chapters abbesses, vicars and others whose lives have been connected in one way or another with the abbey have appeared briefly on the scene. Too often we know nothing of them except their names and a few brief details.

This chapter offers glimpses of one or two characters and historic occasions connected with the abbey and then selects a few longer portraits of people across the centuries who are of interest or have made their mark. The final chapter will dwell more on the ordinary people of Romsey for whom the abbey has been and is their parish church, as they use it for their individual needs and their communal celebrations.

The Glimpses

Some characters have already emerged from the pages of this book, even though we know few hard facts other than those already recorded. For instance, from the days of the nunnery, we have already had a glimpse of the autocratic abbess, Alice Walerand, living in aristocratic style in her lodgings with her pets and her fine fare, and have heard her rebuked for spending money and appointing officials without consulting the chapter.

Again, from the time of the civil war, the parish registers paint a picture of the scholarly Anthony White, poring over his books, as he grieves over the suppression of his beloved prayer book and tries to ignore the sound of cannon shot outside the church or the rabble of Roundheads within, but we know nothing more about him from other sources.

There has been mention, of course, of men of national fame such as Sir William Petty, Lord Palmerston and, from recent times, Lord Mountbatten.

The abbey is proud of its connections with them, but their biographies lie outside the scope of this book.

Royal Visitors

After a long pause, royal visits have been renewed in modern times through the connections of Lord Mountbatten and his grandson, Lord Romsey. In Anglo-Saxon and Norman times, while the seat of government was in Winchester, contact between the nunnery and the monarchy was very close. Festive occasions frequently warranted the presence of the king. We may also picture King Edgar, sorrowing at the death of his young son, but comforted that he lay in a peaceful spot by the river Test with the nuns to pray for his soul (see p.5).

The Norman kings continued their patronage and would sometimes dine at Romsey before embarking for Normandy from Southampton, or would send bucks from their New Forest hunting ground, or a magnum of wine, to celebrate the election of a new abbess. There was also the famous occasion when King Edward I visited the abbey in 1306 and his retainers stayed in the medieval house close by, known today as King John's House, where their graffiti are still incised in the walls.

Visit of King James I

Direct contacts with the crown became less frequent after the capital of the country moved to London. The intended visit of Henry VIII was cancelled because of an outbreak of plague in the town. Queen Elizabeth I passed through Romsey at least once on her progresses to Salisbury or Southampton. A large coat of arms, until recently owned by Whitbread's Brewery commemorated her presence in the town. Whether she visited the abbey church is not recorded, but she never failed to attend divine service, wherever she was.

King James I's visit in August 1607 is, however, memorable for several reasons. Earlier that year he had signed the charter of Romsey's incorporation and its citizens doubtless were anxious to fête him. He chose for the date of his visit the seventh anniversary of the Gowry conspiracy (when two brothers had unsuccessfully plotted to assassinate the king in order to avenge their father's death), and he summoned his favourite bishop, the saintly Lancelot Andrewes, at that time bishop of Chichester, to preach the commemorative sermon.

The ascetic bishop must have contrasted sharply with the raffish, carelessly-dressed king. James is said to have appeared corpulent because his clothes were thickly quilted so as to be dagger proof. It may have been the Gowry conspiracy which caused him to fear the assassin's knife.

The monarch is said to have been accompanied by his queen, Anne of Denmark, and their children, including the future King Charles I, then a boy of seven. Some forty years later the unfortunate King Charles rode through Romsey again, this time under escort, as he was taken from his imprisonment at Hurst Castle to Winchester and thence to London for trial and execution.

In 1607, however, the young Charles would have had no worries except how to sit still for more than an hour while Bishop Andrewes preached on the text:

> And Cushi answered, The enemies of my lord the king, and all
> that rise against thee to do thee hurt, be as that young man is.
> (2 Sam.xviii.32)[1]

'That young man' of course was Absalom who plotted against his father, King David, and was hanged on an oak. The bishop firmly believed in the Divine Right of Kings and, holy man though he was, thought that any who plotted treason should receive their just deserts. The news that Cushi brought was the wretched end of Absalom and the bishop's prayer was that all the king's enemies might likewise perish.

An interesting sidelight on this royal visit to Romsey is the story that the queen used the occasion to steal some of the abbey's treasures. At that time some of the nunnery buildings were still standing and it is recorded that King James had granted a patent for Mary Middlemore, maid of honour to Queen Anne, to search for treasure among the ruins of the abbeys of Romsey, Bury St.Edmunds and Glastonbury.[2] One may well wonder what she found and removed at that time.

PORTRAITS OF PEOPLE

1. Mary de Blois, Abbess of Romsey c.1156-1160

We return to the twelfth century for the first of three short biographies, one of an abbess and two of vicars. Mary was the daughter of King Stephen and Queen Matilda and became a pawn in the political manoeuvres of Henry II when he swept her out of her nunnery and into marriage in spite of the protests of Thomas Becket. She thus unwittingly caused the first rift between the king and his chancellor. On that occasion Henry's anger subsided once he had got his way, but a simmering resentment may have contributed to the later breach with Becket when the full force of the king's fury was directed against him after he became archbishop and championed the rights of the Church against the throne.

The princess was dedicated to the religious life as a child by her mother, two of whose children had already died in infancy. She was placed in the priory of Stratford-atte-Bow, east of London, but the queen, who had been countess of Boulogne until Stephen's seizure of the throne, brought a group of nuns from the convent of St.Sulpice at Rennes to accompany her daughter to the priory and attend to her upbringing. Not surprisingly, friction arose between the two sets of nuns and, as soon as Mary was old enough, Queen Matilda founded a new priory for the St.Sulpice nuns on land which she owned at Lillechurch in Kent. The young princess, still no more than sixteen years of age, was placed at their head as the first prioress. The queen had previously made over the rents from this manor to the Stratford priory in order to cover the expenses of Mary and the foreign nuns. The breakdown in relationships can be read between the lines in a charter of 1150-1152, signed by Archbishop Theobald, the queen and others, by which the nuns of Stratford abandoned all claims to the manor of Lillechurch on condition that the St.Sulpice nuns and their royal charge left Stratford for good with all their belongings and baggage[3].

The Move to Romsey

Previous authorities have stated[4] that we do not know why Mary left the Lillechurch priory for Romsey or whether it happened in Stephen's lifetime (he died in 1154). In fact, it is clear from the dates of charters issued by Henry II that she moved to Romsey some time between 1156 and 1158. (The evidence will be found in Appendix Five.) There may have been difficulties at Lillechurch with the French nuns, but the more likely reason is that by electing a royal princess as abbess the Romsey nunnery would secure more patronage for the building of the church. Mary's uncle, the bishop of Winchester, may have had a hand in the move.

The Scandal of the Marriage

Mary was still very young when elected abbess: she was probably born in 1136, in which case she was only twenty years old. An abbess was supposed to be at least twenty-one, but dispensations were sometimes given. She was not left long in peace to carry out her duties. In the autumn of 1159 her brother William died, leaving her the sole surviving heir to her family's estates, including the wealthy county of Boulogne. Henry II, who was engaged in constant struggle with King Louis of France, wanted to strengthen his continental alliances and in 1160 offered the young abbess's hand in marriage to Matthew of Alsace, younger son of the count of Flanders.

Most medieval chroniclers only state the bald facts of the marriage, but Becket's horror at the enormity of the sacrilege involved in the marriage of an abbess is recorded by several[5]. Exactly how the abbess was conveyed from her convent is not explained. All accounts except one assume that it was against her will. That exception, which describes her as a willing accomplice, implies that she may have been led astray by some kind of special pleading[6]. The forcible abduction of a desirable bride was not uncommon in those times when all feudal marriages were dictated by interests of land and alliances and women were considered to be little more than chattels to be bargained over. The abduction of the abbess would be quite in keeping with this attitude and Henry's autocratic character.

What is undeniable is that Mary, who was normally gentle by nature, was, after her marriage, implacably hostile towards Henry. At one stage she sent a message to his enemy, the French king, warning him of Henry's plots and urging him in the strongest terms to act, *lest the fraudulent king's impetuous presumption should cause you injury*[7]

For all these reasons the present writer has come to disagree with the opinion that Mary could have avoided the match if she had been determined to do so[8].

Mary's later history

When the marriage came to the ears of the pope, he directed his anger against Matthew, first excommunicating him and then placing the county of Boulogne under an interdict until the count should return his bride to her convent. Mary's name, however, was never included in the sentence of excommunication pronounced in this and subsequent papal bulls, which suggests that the pope himself considered that the unfortunate ex-abbess was the victim of an abduction and not herself to blame.

Count Matthew remained obdurate for nine years, ignoring all ecclesiastical censure. Finally —possibly influenced by the fact that Mary had born him two daughters but no heir, and also perhaps moved by his father's death-bed reproof— he yielded to pressure and permitted the unfortunate Mary to retire to a convent at Montreuil. She lived in seclusion there until her early death in 1182 at the age of forty-five.

The effigy of Count Matthew in full armour, a tall and imposing figure, may still be seen in the castle museum at Boulogne. Mary has no memorial unless the tradition is correct that the two little heads on a capital in the south transept of Romsey Abbey represent the ill-fated Mary and her father, King Stephen.

There is little doubt that the marriage of the abbess caused a scandal which rocked the abbey for some time. There seems to have been a long delay before another abbess was elected. Some years later, King Henry, perhaps in remorse for the part he had played in the affair, sent over some nuns from the large and flourishing community at Fontevrault to strengthen the discipline and morale of Romsey Abbey.

2. The Tragic Drowning of Joseph Avery
Vicar of Romsey 1626-?1634

The seventeenth century was a troubled period for the Church with struggles between the Puritans and the High Church faction and conceivably there may have been some dispute over Avery's appointment as vicar of Romsey. At any rate, he seems to have been anxious to make clear that he was a properly ordained clergyman of the Church of England and that he had fulfilled the obligation on all clergy, on taking a new living, of 'reading himself in', by which was meant the public reading and assent to the 39 Articles of Religion. In the parish register for 29 July 1626 we find the following carefully recorded entry:

> *Joseph Avery, minister, took possession of the church of Rumsey as vicar of the place. Item, that the same Joseph Avery did read the book of the Articles the next Sabbath following, being the 30th day of the same month.*

Who was Avery? He came from a Berkshire family and had taken his degree at St. Edmund Hall, Oxford in 1621. We know that he was a strict Puritan, as were many of the parish clergy at that time. Even if he met with opposition from some quarters, no doubt most people in Romsey were content with the prevailing type of protestant worship of those days — a central communion table, said prayers, the singing of rhymed versions of the psalms, a long sermon and rigid sabbatarianism — and would have had no objection to the ministry of the zealous young Puritan. However, when William Laud became Archbishop of Canterbury in 1633, he set out to restore the Catholic tradition in the Church of England and put great pressure on the Puritan clergy, suspending or depriving many who would not conform.

As a result of persecution, some 20,000 Puritans emigrated to New England between 1630 and 1640 and among them in 1634, went Parson Avery, his wife and six children, together with his cousin and great friend, Antony Thacher, and his family. As young men, the two friends had formed *a league of perpetual friendship* promising *to be partakers of each other's misery or welfare, as also of habitation in the same place.*

125

The party landed safely at Boston, Massachusetts and travelled northwards to the small town of Newbury at the mouth of the Merrimack river, where they had relatives in the local church.

What happened next is best told in the words of Professor S.E.Morison of Harvard University who researched the tragic events in Massachusetts Bay[9]:

> *The two friends had not been very long at Newbury before Avery was persuaded that it was his duty to bring the light of the Gospel to the godless fishermen of Marblehead; when he so decided the Thachers, by virtue of the compact, must accompany him. On an August day in 1635, the two families set sail from Ipswich in an open pinnace. There were eleven Averys, including children and servants, nine Thachers, one more passenger, and some livestock. The passage to Marblehead, a matter of only thirty-five miles, is commonly made nowadays by small racing yachts without the slightest trouble. But this ship's company had the bad luck to set forth on the evening of one of the worst summer tempests that ever struck the New England coast —one that blew down hundreds of trees, overthrew houses and 'drave great ships from their anchors'. First the wind blew hard from the south-west and split all the sails, as the pinnace was just off Cape Ann. The rest of the course lying to windward, the mariners decided to anchor until daylight. At midnight the wind whipped around to the north-east, the anchor came home, and the pinnace dragged and drifted on to a small barren rock, where it lodged fast, the rapidly-rising seas breaking over her and tearing everything loose. All the children were swept off and drowned. Mrs Thacher happened to be on the scuttle or quarter-deck when that part of the ship broke away, and safely floated her ashore. Avery and Thacher, expecting any moment to be washed away, said farewell to one another, and Avery prayed aloud:*

>> *'We know not what the Pleasure of God is; I fear we have been too unmindful of former Deliverances: Lord, I cannot challenge a promise of the Preservation of my Life; but thou hast promised to deliver us from Sin and Condemnation, and to bring us safe to Heaven, through the All-sufficient Satisfaction of Jesus Christ; this therefore do I challenge of thee.'*

126

No sooner was this said than a wave swept Avery off the rock and he was seen no more. Another wave took the rest of the Thachers. Only the father managed to grasp a piece of wreckage, with which he drifted ashore to an island, where he found his wife. By great good fortune, a knapsack containing flint, steel, and a powder horn was cast ashore, together with two cheeses and a drowned goat; and there was a spring on the island, so the Thachers were able to subsist through the tempest, until a passenger ship rescued them. Antony and his wife survived to found a famous New England family of divines and lawyers, but the entire Avery family was wiped out. And as practically all their property was on board the pinnace, there was nothing left of their estate but a sow and pigs and ten bushels of corn.

Antony named the island of his deliverance 'Thacher's Island' and the rock where the ship struck 'Avery his Fall'.

Two centuries after Avery's death the American Quaker poet, J.G.Whittier, commemorated his story in a ballad called "The Swan Song of Parson Avery". One verse runs:

The ear of God was open to his servant's last request;
As the strong wave swept him downward the sweet hymn
upward pressed,
And the soul of Father Avery went, singing, to its rest.

Winthrop, the Puritan Governor of Connecticut in Avery's day, described him as 'a precious, holy minister'. His memory is still honoured on the shores of Boston Bay where he went to preach the Gospel and it is right that he should still be remembered in Romsey where his ministry began.

3. The Rev. E.L.Berthon, Vicar 1860-1892

We move forward another two centuries to the long incumbency of the Rev. Edward Lyon Berthon, whose name has already cropped up several times in this book. He was a remarkable man whose life-span matched that of Queen Victoria whom he much admired. He was typical of the Victorian ruling class who had the means and leisure to follow their own pursuits. At a time when manufacturers and traders prospered and spread their network

127

The Rev. E. L. Berthon

worldwide, many of these Victorians were intrepid travellers, energetic, confident of their superiority and proud of their nation and its achievements. Berthon shared these attributes, but was outstanding in his generation for his enquiring and inventive mind. We know about his family and background from the autobiography which he wrote when in his eighties[10].

Edward Lyon Berthon was born in 1813, the tenth child of the family. His mother was the daughter of a famous surgeon and his father was a prosperous businessman, but descended from the French Huguenot nobility. Family fortunes plunged when Waterloo and the hastily concluded peace which followed ended his father's contracts to supply the army; at the same time a convoy of his ships was wrecked off Portugal. Berthon described this disaster as a descent from affluence to comparative poverty, but 'comparative' is the operative word as throughout his life lack of money never seems to have prevented him from extensive travelling or from funding his various projects and inventions.

His memories of schooldays were of harsh discipline, poor food and an education based on Latin and Greek which provided no stimulus for his scientific turn of mind nor recognition of his artistic talent. His first intention was to follow his maternal grandfather as a surgeon, a vocation which required a strong stomach in the days before anaesthetics were discovered. After an apprenticeship in Liverpool he went to Dublin to complete his training at the Royal College of Surgeons.

Something of his zest for life is revealed when he looked back in old age at the hazards of travel in the first half of the century while sitting for two nights and a day on the box of the mail between London and Holyhead before embarking for Kingstown on some wretched little steamboat. In memory, at any rate, he could forget the discomforts and remembered only,

> the spanking teams of nearly thoroughbred horses, with their bright and beautiful harness; the lively guards and coachmen, with their red coats and long tin horns; and the wayside inns, where Guard would say, "Twenty minutes here for dinner, gentlemen."

> Changing horses in the last of the coaching days was a thing to be remembered. We drove up at a gallop between the fresh horses, each held by a man, who took out the tired team and put others in their

129

places in a few seconds. The coachman threw the reins down, caught the new ones, and we were off again to the music of the horn in less than a minute.

Sometimes an amusing adventure would add to the delights of travelling. One cold moonlight night I had to go, with two of my sisters, by the mail from Liverpool to Bangor. On Penmaenmawr there was deep snow, and we got off the road. The coach was nearly wheels uppermost in a ditch; and all the "outsides" were catapulted into a snowdrift, from which we could hardly scramble out for laughing.[11]

Berthon's studies in Dublin came to a sudden end when he became seriously ill with pneumonia. While in Liverpool he had become engaged and after his recovery it was decided that the marriage should take place forthwith so that the newly-wed couple could holiday together on the continent.

After travelling through several countries, they stayed for a while in furnished apartments in Rome, where his wife had a very genteel lady's maid, from whom Berthon learnt Italian while she dressed his wife's hair. Their meals were brought from the local trattoria in a large tin box with a charcoal fire in it. They went frequently to the opera where they had a box. Eventually, they moved on to Naples and Sorrento, returned to Rome for Easter, and in 1835 came back to winter at Bangor.

Everywhere Berthon went he was observant and his mind was busy with inventions. During a trip on the lake of Geneva he conceived the idea of a screw propellor and back in Bangor he made a model steamboat to try out his theory. The Admiralty dismissed it as a "pretty toy" with no future in it and Berthon abandoned the venture, only to find that another inventor had lit on the same idea which was afterwards adopted by the navy.

The couple next settled for a while on the Isle of Wight where their first child was born. It was now his wife's turn to succumb to ill-health and they embarked on another spell abroad, this time accompanied by nurse and child as well. Their travels lasted altogether for six years, but in 1841 Berthon, having decided to take Holy Orders, went to Cambridge to take his degree. After a curacy at Lymington, he was presented to a living in Fareham. Two years later he went to Jersey for six months to recover from bronchitis and used his time there for perfecting an invention for indicating the speed of ships. He was invited to Windsor to explain his invention to the Prince Consort. The queen was so impressed that she ordered his indicators to be fitted to the royal yachts. All went well until two years later when the queen was aboard the 'Victoria and Albert' and the indicator recorded that the yacht had begun to lose speed. The captain maintained that the indicator had become unreliable and the queen ordered its removal. By the time that it was discovered that the engine and not the indicator was to blame, Berthon's patent had run out and once again he earned nothing from his invention.

Over a period, Berthon was involved in various other nautical inventions, such as a clinometer or trim indicator, a roll indicator and draft indicator, none of which gained him much recognition until he invented his collapsible lifeboats, but even then his first attempts to promote them ended in failure.

The invention was inspired by the sinking of a passenger ship, the 'SS Orion', off Ireland. Loss of life was heavy because of the lack of lifeboats and Berthon hit on the idea of making boats with longitudinal timbers, jointed together at the ends and covered with canvas, which would fold down like the leaves of a book. Again he failed to interest the Admiralty in his invention. He graphically describes how the queen summoned him to demonstrate his boat. He was sailing his thirty foot craft alone one afternoon on the Serpentine in London when he was hailed from the shore by a man with a large envelope. It proved to be a summons from the queen to be at Osborne with the boat at 11.0 am the next morning. Berthon's panache and resourcefulness are well illustrated in what followed:

> *All my men had returned to Fareham, but, fortunately, two pairs of wheels which carried the boat were on the bank. I ran to the Receiving House of the Royal Humane Society and borrowed men. One of these I sent to fetch three cabs with all speed, whilst the others collapsed the boat — she weighed twenty-six hundredweight — and put her on her wheels. When the cabs came I said, "I only want your horses, here are ropes, harness them, and if you reach Nine Elms in time for the 6 pm goods train, you shall have ten shillings apiece." Away they went at a gallop. I went down to Gosport by the mail train and found the boat at the station. Next morning I mustered a fine crew of twelve watermen, all in their Sunday blue. At 10 am the boat was afloat,*

masts stepped, and sails hoisted. A nice breeze took us over to Osborne in forty-five minutes.

Punctually at eleven o'clock the royal carriage arrived at the beach ... Her Majesty expressed her admiration and asked me many pertinent questions.[12]

Although the queen was impressed, the Admiralty again failed to back the project. Berthon was so disgusted at his treatment that he decided to resign his living at Fareham and turn his back on boats and the sea for good.

Not long afterwards, he was offered the living of Romsey and began a ministry which was to last for more than thirty years. He found a new interest and outlet for his talents in the restoration of the great Norman church and delighted in the hospitality he received from Lord Palmerston at Broadlands and the company of the men of distinction whom he met there.

Unfortunately, by 1864 his wife's health had deteriorated to such an extent that he was recommended to take her abroad. By the following spring it had become clear that there was no hope of recovery and they returned to Romsey so that she could die, as she wished, in her own home. Death was soon also to remove Berthon's ally, Lord Palmerston, from the scene.

Unexpectedly, thirteen years after moving to Romsey, with new men in the Admiralty, a new interest was expressed in Berthon's collapsible boats. He set up a boat-yard in the town and was soon receiving orders on a large scale. He was also able to promote his collapsible pontoons and portable hospitals. His interests were unlimited and extended as well into astronomy for which he invented a number of improvements for telescopes. A boatyard in Lymington still bears his name.

The restoration of the abbey church provided Berthon with a different challenge. Some of his achievements have already been recorded (see Chapter Seven). Some owed their success to the existence of the boat-yard and his own inventive genius. When he moved the organ and choir from a gallery in the north transept to the chancel, he was able to use a skilled carver who worked in the boat-yard to decorate the new choir stalls with heads of English kings and queens, bishops and abbesses to match the row

132

of medieval carved heads which he had placed on a new screen across the chancel.

Two other projects provided a challenge for his skill and inventiveness. The first was the repair of the north transept roof for which he adapted boat-building techniques, as he himself describes:[13]

> *The span of this roof is thirty-four feet, and the principals are large semicircular arches, one foot in depth and ten inches wide. In the usual way these would be cut out of the solid, in short lengths, and joined together, which is expensive, involving great waste of timber, and very much labour. So I resolved to make them as I do the gunwales and timbers of my boats, viz. by bending twelve one-inch planks, one over another, and riveting them together. The planks being of varying widths to suit the proper section, very little work was needed to mould them to the required form. At the intersection of these carved principals with the purlins are large gilt bosses, ornamented with leaves all different; all these and all the gilt paterae on the cornices are the work of my own hands.*

The other test of Berthon's ingenuity came when the lower arches east of the altar were opened. It was then found that instead of framing the east windows in the retrochoir, as had clearly been intended, the windows were exposed to view 'with their heads cut off'. The windows are in the Decorated style, matching the large east windows above the high altar and they were moved back into the east wall when the Lady chapel was demolished after the Dissolution. Berthon wrote[14]:

> *Those early Protestant churchwardens, whose only idea was to keep out wind and rain, had reset these beautiful windows so high up that there was no room for the sixfoil circles in the old archways.*

He seems to have been unaware that the real reason for the awkward positioning was to leave room below for an entrance into the present St. Mary's chapel. This door had remained in use for several centuries, but had been blocked up when replaced by an entrance at the eastern end of the north wall.

Chancel showing retrochoir windows before they were lowered by Berthon and sixfoils restored

Berthon tackled the job with his customary ingenuity. Each window weighed at least a ton and they had to be cut clear of the surrounding masonry and kept vertical in order not to break the glass while they were lowered about two feet. Employing four unskilled labourers and using four specially designed screws, he claimed to have completed the work in three hours with not a pane of glass broken. New sixfoils were added to complete the tracery at the top. They are so well-made that they are indistinguishable from the original work.

From a private letter written by Charles Spence, it is clear that Berthon would have liked to have gone further in restoring the abbey church to its original design. In particular, he would have liked to open up again the two circular chapels to the transepts and to have built a new belfry so that the tower would once again have been open to its roof. Undoubtedly the church would have gained architecturally, but the practical problems were too enormous even for Berthon to solve.

Charles Spence, who knew personally both Berthon and Gerard Noel, his predecessor, when called on by his correspondent to make a comparison between the two men, praised Noel for cleaning off all the whitewash, removing the unsightly west gallery and restoring stonework and described

134

him as having seen a glimpse of fine art in the church, but he declared that it was Berthon, more highly gifted, who had the vision to restore its full glorious panorama.[15]

Noel was undoubtedly the better-loved of the two clergymen. He was known as the Good Vicar and when he died many of the Romsey shops were kept partially closed until after the funeral as a mark of affection and respect. Caroline, his youngest daughter who is commemorated in a window and tablet in the south aisle, composed the fine hymn with the opening lines,

> *At the name of Jesus*
> *Every knee shall bow,*

and she shared her father's faith and devotion. Berthon, on the other hand, suffered from no false modesty about his very real achievements, and his failures in dealing with the lords of the Admiralty were possibly due in part to a lack of tact which made them resent the interfering parson who tried to teach them their job. However, even though he was absent from the parish for long spells during his ministry, so that a joke circulated about his boat-building interests:

> *St.Peter forsook his boats for the Church: Berthon forsook the*
> *Church for his boats!*

He seems to have been popular, especially with the children. In spite of the small population of the town, he had three curates and there was a full programme of services: twice daily in the abbey (with four or five services on Sundays); twice weekly in a mission room in Middlebridge Street and at Crampmoor; and once or twice every Sunday in the chapels at Lee and Ridge. Some of his projects, such as the pavilion to seat 2,500 people which he erected in the Market Place on the occasion of the Prince of Wales' marriage, were for the benefit of the whole community.

The many societies reflect the social conditions of the time. In addition to Mothers' meetings and Sunday Schools, there was a District Visiting Society; a Temperance Society; a Penny Clothing Club; a Dorcas Society; a Loan Blanket Society; a Working Men's Society; the Guild of Nazareth for boys and a Girls' Friendly Society. There were also various groups to support home and foreign missions.

135

PAVILION ERECTED IN THE MARKET PLACE, ROMSEY, BY REV. E. L. BERTHON, WHEN 2,5(
PERSONS DINED TOGETHER ON THE OCCASION OF THE MARRIAGE OF H.R.H. THE
PRINCE OF WALES, MARCH 10TH, 1863. (FROM A DRAWING BY REV. E. L. B.)

Within the abbey, Berthon did much to restore a sense of reverence and good order in worship. He was constantly exhorting the congregation to kneel and not sit during prayers and to arrive in good time to secure their places. Matins at 11.0 am was the main service and the litany was used every Sunday and twice during the week. Like Queen Victoria, whom he so much admired, he must have become almost an institution when he finally retired in his eightieth year.

REFERENCES

1. L. Andrewes, *Ninety-six Sermons* (Oxford 1841)
2. C. Spence, MS notes, p.58
3. A. Saltman, *Theobald, Archbishop of Canterbury*, pp.379-380
4. Coldicott p.33, Liveing p.55
5. Matt. West. II, p.45; Herbert, quoted Bouquet, XIV, p.454
6. M.Everett Green, *Princesses of England*, vol.I, p.197 footnote
7. Bouquet, XVI, p.144
8. Coldicott, p.33; Walker, p.14
9. Recounted in St.Edmund Hall magazine, Oxford 1935
10. Berthon, *A Retrospect of Eight Decades*
11. Ib. pp.33-34
12. Ib. pp.127-128
13. Ib. p.157
14. Ib. p.159

CHAPTER TWELVE

THE LITTLE TOWN WITH THE LARGE CHURCH

This final chapter looks at Romsey, the small market town left with the responsibility of caring for the great abbey church. No wonder if at times the building has been looked on as more of a liability than a legacy.

Romsey at the Reformation

Between Norman times and the dissolution of the nunnery, Romsey had gradually undergone a transformation. In the Domesday survey all the land was owned by the abbey and the population consisted of 39 villeins and 53 bordars (small-holders) who worked their land as tenants, plus two slaves who had no land but received protection, food and shelter in return for their labour. These men and their families made up the small farming community and lived in thatched hovels, sparsely furnished with perhaps a straw mattress, a board for a table, a stool or two, some pots and pans and a few home-made tools.

By Tudor times, Romsey had grown and prospered as a small but thriving market town, primarily as a result of its sizable wool and clothing trade. At the dissolution the citizens were ready to assume the mantle of responsibility and manage their own affairs independently of the nunnery. Doubtless feelings were mixed about the suppression of the abbey, but it no longer played an essential part in the life of the town. Labourers who had been directly employed by it may have been the losers, but abbey officials had the foresight to apply for annuities and leases and many men were able to increase their personal fortunes through the release of land and tenements.

Wills and inventories give us a vivid insight into the life of the community in the Tudor period[1]. There was reluctance to make a will until one was at death's door, in spite of the Church's teaching that it was sinful not to do so. The common people were superstitious and believed that to make a will while still in good health was tempting Providence, so many who met with sudden death must have died intestate. Most wills, therefore, were made when the testator was *in extremis*. He sent usually for his parish priest who would urge him for the good of his soul to pay his debts, make a gift to the

Church and provide for his family. The vicar is often a witness to wills of this period and no doubt frequently penned them on the testator's behalf.

The wills begin by affirming that the testator, although sick in body is 'whole of mind and of perfect remembrance'. He nearly always leaves something 'for tithes forgotten'. (In spite of the 'perfect remembrance', tithes were very often conveniently forgotten during a man's lifetime, but pricked his conscience when about to meet his Maker.)

After the testator's death, a very careful inventory was made of his goods; it is by such inventories that we are able to walk through each room of a man's house and observe how he lived. For instance, the barber, Simon Alyn, lived in a one-up, one-down, but was comfortably supplied with a good store of provisions. In the hall he has only a table and cupboard, three platters, three pottengers and two saucers, along with his armoury of sword, dagger and bow; but he also has in store:

> *j hogge, iij flytchis of bacon, iij breast of beefe, ij old tubbes and ij quarter of wheat.*

Bettrixe Burnham was apparently a well-to-do widow, for her house consisted of a hall, buttery, kitchen, three chambers and a servant's room. The servant was Alice Miller to whom she left her 'second petticoat'. She had cupboards and chairs, cushions and curtains, as well as two kine and a sow hog.

Not all were so prosperous. Our hearts bleed for poor Richard Goldering who dies in penury. For the sake of his soul he leaves 2d. to his mother church of St.Swithun and 2d. to his parish church and would like to make provision for his wife:

> *but as God knows my debts to be sore, I fear she shall enjoy no part of it.*

He can only pray his ghostly father to see that his poor body is given Christian burial.

Such are the details in these inventories that we can see the kitchen where some old dame kept *'an old kettel'* and *'ij potts of grease'*, or was the proud owner of *'a spittle, pothangers, andirons and frypan'*. We also walk with these

139

ghosts of the past down the familiar streets of 'Mydill Brige' and 'Portesbrige' or to 'Cherfylle Streete' and 'ye Causeway'. At its heart, Romsey is the same little market town now which our forefathers knew.

Religious Confusion

In the wills of the late fifteenth and early sixteenth centuries people were clear about their religious duties. They begin their wills, *'I bequeath my soul to Almighty God, our Lady St.Mary and to the whole company of heaven'*. They leave money to the Brotherhood of St.George for obits to be said for their souls, and they leave small sums or a quantity of wax for lights to burn at the shrines of their favourite saints. Reference has already been made to the sums of money left 'for tithes forgotten'. That religious duty persisted after the abbey's dissolution, but parishioners might be forgiven for some confusion over what else they ought to do to ensure their salvation amid the conflicting doctrines of the times.

During the brief reforming reign of Edward VI, lights before altars and requests for obits are usually dropped in favour of bequests of alms for the poor, but John Blowes, who died in 1549, still longs for an obit and requests his wife to bestow yearly half the rent of one of his houses

> *for an obit for me and my friends in my parish church in Romsey **if it may be lawfully kept;** if not, to be distributed to the poor.*

Bettrixe Burnham, already mentioned, who died just after Elizabeth I succeeded the Catholic Mary on the throne, is still sure that an obit is in order and asks her son to keep a yearly one for her in her parish church. Later in the century, under the Elizabethan settlement, Thomas Browne, evidently a man of substance, states firmly:

> *I trust to be saved by the shedding of the most precious blood of the Saviour and by no other means.*

Similar phrases appear in many other wills.

Mostly, these post-dissolution testators seem to have realized the responsibility which lay on them, after the nuns had departed, to maintain

140

and repair their parish church and small sums are frequently left for *'reparacions'*. Maud Cradock, however, is determined that the church shall only receive money when it requires it; she leaves 3s.4d. to be paid by her executor *'when he shall see it needful to be bestowed'*.

Decline and depression

The period of prosperity in Romsey when yeomen farmers and petty merchants were able to bequeath lands and leases, tenements and orchards, money and goods to their families, was short-lived. It was soon replaced by a downward drift to decline and depression. Some individuals, of course, made money out of recession, but by and large the wool trade, on which the town had depended, went into a slow decline over the next three centuries and never fully recovered. The loss of Calais, where the wool staple functioned, dealt a blow to the English exporters and other problems followed. In 1586 we hear of a great dearth and want of work which was causing unrest and unlawful assemblies of the common people.

Because the clothing trade depended on small-scale industry, there was no great capital behind it to cushion it against competition or periods of recession. A century later the Act for Burying in Wool (1678) was recorded in the parish register. It was intended to increase the demand for wool in the face of competition from linen imported from Ireland and one man at least is believed to have benefited from it. He was John Vanderplank from a Flemish Huguenot family who died in 1717. His tombstone is in the nave of the abbey church. He was a master clothier who left more than £600, a sizable fortune in those days.[2]

In general, however, the fulling and dyeing of wool, once Romsey's main industry, was in decline and those engaged in it no longer prospered. At about the same period, Sir William Petty's father, Anthony, who was a clothier, in spite of living in a spacious merchant's house, was perpetually burdened by debt. Romsey still maintained its reputation for manufacturing excellent shalloons (a light woollen material) in the mid-eighteenth century, although by the end of the century that industry too had almost disappeared and manufacture was limited to sacks and paper.

Civic Sense

Within twenty years of the dissolution we hear mention of a mayor and constables in Romsey[3], and the familiar 'portcullis' seal dates back to 1578. When King James I granted borough status to Romsey in a charter of 1607, it was decreed that a common council should be formed consisting of the mayor, six aldermen and twelve capital burgesses. John Stork, who was already mayor under the old system, was to act as 'modern' mayor until the election of a new one.[4] The duties of this body were unpaid and citizens were not always anxious to be elected, but a fine could be imposed on those who refused to serve.

A few years before the granting of the charter, the bishop had discovered that the church building was in a sorry state and had ordered the churchwardens to carry out repairs. It was probably in order that there should be a properly constituted body to assist them in this task that he agreed that twenty persons of the parish should have the government and direction of the church and 'all goods and stock pertaining thereto'[5] - an early forerunner of the parochial church council. With a council established for church matters and a mayor and corporation for civic affairs, the little town may be said to have come of age.

The Seventeenth and Eighteenth Centuries

Romsey grew very slowly through these two centuries and by 1900 the population was still only in the region of 5,000. A small number of its citizens rose to great prosperity and were benefactors to the poor, such as John Kent and John Bartlett, commemorated in the almshouses which bear their names as well as in memorials to them in the church. Sir William Petty (see p.86) and John Jacob (a maltster's son who wrote poetry as well as compiling a law dictionary) left their home town and achieved eminence on the national stage.

In general, however, the sleepy market town went about its own small business and only woke to bustling activity on market days and at the annual fairs. There was pride in the past, but a helpless inability to maintain a parish church which was larger than many cathedrals, and there was little knowledge or appreciation of its history and architecture.

One may smile at some of the contrivances and contraptions dictated by economy, but where were the funds for the upkeep of such a building? Largely they had to come from an unpopular church rate and from pew rents. Sir William Petty reckoned that the population of the town was virtually static at about 2,700 between the reigns of Elizabeth I and Charles I. By the end of the eighteenth century it was about 4,000.

View of the abbey from the Test, dated 1777

143

1800-1900: A century of little change

We may compare two pictures of the town, a century apart but easily recognizable as the same town. A directory of 1798[6] describes Romsey as follows:

> *A large market for corn etc. is held here every Saturday: here are also three fairs, viz. on Easter-Monday, the 26th of August, and the 8th of November, principally for cattle, cheese and toys.*

> *The principle staple articles of this town are sacks, paper and beer; it once carried on a large trade in the woollen manufactory, but it is now greatly diminished.*

Here is an almshouse for six poor widows; a charity-school for thirty, and a free-school for ten boys.

It then gives the principal inhabitants of Romsey Infra. After listing the mayor and corporation, other officials, four physicians and two attorneys, it names 145 residents and gives their occupations. Romsonians, familiar with the old saying, 'so drunk, he must have been to Romsey', will not be surprised to learn that innkeepers are the largest single group (19); all other providers of food and drink total twenty-three. The clothing trade, including seven cordwainers (shoemakers) and two slopsellers (who sold ready-made clothes) accounted for twenty people. Another fifty were occupied in a variety of trades (brazier, cooper, blacksmith, wheelwright, tanner, stonemason, coachmaker etc.). The remaining twenty-two offered services of various kinds, such as bankers, postmaster, gardeners, carriers and schoolmasters. The rest of the population was presumably made up of their families and of unskilled labourers, some of whom would have worked for the six people listed as paper and sack manufacturers.

Compare that picture of Romsey with the vivid account written by an elderly lady in 1979 as she remembered what the town was like early in this century. The changes are not so very great:

> *When I was a child, Romsey was a small market town with a population of less than 5,000. We were almost self supporting, with our very own gas works, brewery, jam factory, flour and paper mills,*

printers, boat builders and tannery. We were the proud possessors of a town band, town crier and a fire engine which could not attend until 'steam was up'. We had a saddler, cabinet maker, upholsterer, blacksmith, clock maker, tailor and costumier.

Romsey was known for its smells ... marmalade in January, strawberry jam in July; not too pleasant smells from the tannery and a healthy smell of hops and malt from the brewery, together with a delicious smell of hot, new, crusty bread and lardy cakes all greasy and gooey. If you happened to be in the streets after 10 pm there would be the 'The Night Cart'.

On winter afternoons one could watch the lamplighter on his bicycle, carrying a long pole, lighting each lamp in turn along the street. Until the second World War the curfew rang at 8 pm and the knell tolled the age of the departed, the name of whom would be posted on the church door.
Thursday was market day; very busy; cows, pigs and sheep could be seen wending their way along the Hundred to the Market Place. Cattle were tethered in the Corn Market.

Tables set up along the pavement edge showed hutches and coops with rabbits and poultry on view prior to the sale. Fresh eggs and butter were always available. Besides the farmers and their waggons were the carriers who brought people from the villages and shopped for others. The fare to Wellow was 1d. but grown ups had to walk up the Pauncefoot Hill.

... We could bowl hoops, bounce balls or skip our way to school (no traffic problems). In February we played marbles in the brim filled gutters and in July, when the sun always shone, we cooled and refreshed ourselves under the spray of the water carts ...

For pleasure and entertainment there was a cricket club and ground in Alma Road and on the opposite side sometimes a fair with swing, roundabouts, steam engines and gingerbread stalls...

145

Saturday evening saw the brakes with their teams of horses and noisy passengers making their way to the drinking houses.

That was Romsey, the little market town.[7]

Celebrations

Because of Romsey's strong sense of civic pride, it always threw itself with great gusto into national and local celebrations in the days when all entertainment was homespun. These celebrations were made possible through the help of the abbey church and its inventive Victorian vicar on one edge of the town and the cooperation of the owners of the Broadlands estate on another. The scale of the celebrations is described in contemporary reports.

Marriage of the Prince of Wales 1863

For this occasion the Rev. E.L.Berthon (see p.135) erected an enormous pavilion in the market place where 2,000 persons (virtually the whole adult population) dined together at long tables. The pavilion even included an upper gallery.

Queen Victoria's Jubilee 1887

For the next celebration Lord Mount Temple put Broadlands at the disposal of the organizing committee and the Berthon Boat Company again erected a tent in the grounds to seat about 2,000 with a band platform at one end. The committee planned the programme with a budget of £300:[8] a thanksgiving service was held in the abbey at 11.15 am, followed by a procession to Broadlands during which all traffic was stopped. All inhabitants over the age of sixteen were invited to the dinner at 2 pm. Catering included 2,000 lbs beef, 1,000 lbs of plum pudding, seven sacks of potatoes and 125 gallons of bread (one wishes that more details survived about the cooking and serving of these great quantities). Later, there was tea for the children who were each presented with a commemorative mug. This was followed by sports and games, with a firework display in the evening and a torchlight procession back into the town.

Sunday School outing 1888

Undeterred by all the work which had gone into celebrating the Queen's Jubilee in the previous year, the clergy organized this outing on an ambitious scale in 1888. It appears to have been an annual event, but only the 1888 copy of the early parish magazines has survived to give an account of it.

After a service in the abbey, 700 children and accompanying adults marched to the railway station led by the town band. A special train took them to Portchester where they were entertained in the castle grounds.

> ...Here were assembled for their sole benefit and amusement gingerbread stalls, shooting galleries, coconut shies, swing boats and all the thousand and one adjuncts which go to make up the sum of a village fair. Chorister boys were soon galloping up and down on ponies ... whilst the little girls crowded round the vendor of some very highly-coloured ices, who was shouting, 'Cooler! cooler! a penn'orth for a 'a'penny!'[9]

Millenary Celebrations 1907

Even more ambitious than the 19th century festivities was the great pageant to commemorate the founding (or re-founding) of the nunnery by Edward the Elder. The grounds of Broadlands were lent by the Rt. Hon. Evelyn Ashley and a covered grandstand was erected on the chosen site near the river. The pageant ran for three days and H.R.H. Princess Louise attended the opening service in the abbey. All profits went to the Abbey Restoration Fund and for the building of a new north porch on the site of the medieval porticus. Town and parish were totally united in the ambitious project which was directed from the Mayor's Parlour and seems to have involved everyone in the community. Research was undertaken, words and music written, costumes made and parts learnt and rehearsed. The Berthon Boat Company made the Danish ships and an Abbey Gateway was constructed.[10]

Recent Times

The ancient borough has not lost its capacity for celebration, even if not on the same expansive scale as in Victorian-Edwardian times. Many occasions fill the old abbey church in a way which would have delighted its Norman builders, and the church for its part still looks to the town for help in maintaining this priceless heritage.

REFERENCES

1. Wills & inventories from transcriptions made by LTVAS
2. Tony Vanderplank, *Romsey Magazine*. August 1980
3. Liveing, p.276
4. Latham, vol.1, p.211
5. C.Spence, MS notebook, p.7
6. *Universal British Directory*, vol.4, 1798, p.352
7. Mrs F.E.Gay, *Romsey Magazine*, May 1975
8. *Hampshire Chronicle*, 11 June 1887
9. *Romsey Magazine*, August 1888
10. Full account published under title *Romsey Millenary Celebrations, A.D. 907-A.D. 1907*

APPENDIX ONE

ABBESSES OF ROMSEY

(Based by kind permission from *Hampshire Nunneries* by Diana K. Coldicott, pp.161-162, where sources are given)

Name, date of election or period when active in office and death, where known.

Elfleda (dau.Edw. the Elder)	10th cent. d. 959 (?)
St.Merewenna	967 x 975
Elwina	? 990's
St.Ethelfleda	? 990's
Wulf(w)ynn	? 11th c.
Elfgyfu	? 11th c.
(Christina ?)	circa 1086
Athelitz	-1102
Hadewidis	1130 x 1133
Matilda	1133 x 1155 d.1155
Mary de Blois	elected ?1156 resigned 1160[1]
Juliana	1174 x 1199 d. 1199
Matilda Patriz (sister of Walter Walerand)	elected 3 June 1199 d. 14 Dec.1230

i

Matilda de Barbeflé d. April 1237	elected 1231
Isabella de Neville	elected April - May 1237 d. (unrecorded)
Cecilia	elected ?1238 signature occurs 1244 d. (unrecorded)
Constance	elected Sept.1247 d. ?1260 (6 months vacancy)
Amicia de Sulhere (Sullye)	elected May - June 1261 d. July 1268
Alice Walerand	elected July 1268 d. April 1298
Philippa de Stokes	elected April 1298 d. Sept.1307
Clementia de Gildeford	elected Sept. - Oct.1307 d. Dec.1314
Alice de Wyntreshull	elected Jan. - Feb.1315 d. May 1315
Sybil Carbonel	elected July - Aug.1315 d. June 1333
Joan Icthe	elected June - July 1333 d. April 1349
Joan Gerveys	elected May 1349 d. Oct.1352
Isabella Cammoys	elected Nov.1352 d. April 1396
Lucy Everard	elected April - May 1396 d. July 1405

ii

Felicia Aas	elected July - Aug.1405 d. October 1417
Matilda Lovell	elected Nov.1417 d. April 1462
Johanna Brygges	elected April - May 1462 d. May 1472
Elizabeth Brooke	elected June 1472 resigned Aug.1478 re-elected Aug. - Oct.1478 d. by 6 June 1502
Joyce Rowse	elected June 1502 resigned Sept.1515
Anne Westbroke	elected Sept. 1515 d. by 1 Dec.1523
Elizabeth Ryprose	electedDec.1523 - Jan.1524 (Abbey dissolved 1539) d. unknown

REFERENCE

1.   See Appendix Five

APPENDIX TWO

VICARS OF ROMSEY

(NB Dates of some early vicars are approximate)

1322	Henry de Chilmark	Vicarage first endowed
1334	Nicholas de Botelston	From Boston, Lincs. Died in Black Death
1349	William de Bures	Died in Black Death
1349	John de Minstede	In 1367 donated lands to Abbey
1371	John Folyot	Famous for dispute with Abbess
1377	Thomas Eggesworth	Investigated dispute; replaced Folyot
1380	Roger Purye	Vicar at time of Peasants' Revolt
1400	John Umfray	Away 3 years while parish church enlarged
c.1428	John Kent	Exchanged benefices with John Bayly of Winchester
1452	John Bayly	Became prebendary in 1452 or a little later
1464	John Greene	Resigned on becoming prebendary of Timsbury
1482	Edward Coleman	Nothing known about him
c.1493	Richard Sclater	1502 nun accused of incontinence with Vicar. He apparently resigned.
c.1502	Thomas Nayle	Bequeathed his red mantle to Agnes Harvey, a nun
c.1505	John Hopwood	1507 Bishop ordered vicar not to enter Abbey precincts
1519	John Newman	Long incumbency spanned period of dissolution
1546	Walter Morys	Appointed by Richard Wynslade. Patronage then passed to dean and chapter, then to bishop
1558	Thomas Chester	1561 Accused of 'popish' practices
1563	Thomas Yaxly	No record of appointment but named as vicar in a will

1567	Edward Walker	Parish records were begun in 1569
1575	Hugh Kingley	Nothing known about him
c.1580	Hugh Richardson	Nothing known about him
1586	Henry Hopkins	Nothing known. Time of depression and unemployment
1589	George Blunt	Resigned after a year, no reason given. Probably became rector of Exton
1590	Samuel Adams	Wealthy man (inventory survives). In 1607 48 Romsey people refused to receive communion
1620	Robert Bostock	Also held appointments at Exton and Mottisfont
1626	Joseph Avery	Emigrated to New England (see p.126)
1637	Anthony White	M.A. from Corpus Christi Oxford. Supporter of Prayer Book abolished by Parliament
1648	John Warren (Intruder)	Not episcopally ordained and ejected after Act of Uniformity
1662	Thomas Doughty	M.A. from Magdalene, Cambridge. Came from Wakefield
1666	James Wood	Died after three years in office
1669	Samuel Wartensius	1671 married Judith Jordan at Timsbury. 2nd marriage to widow, Mrs Fyges
1675	Thomas Donne	M.A. from St. John's Oxford. 777 dissenters recorded in Romsey
1680	Joshua Mitchell	Ordained at Gloucester in 1671
1693	William Mayo	Well-known personality. Married Elizabeth Gollop of Stanbridge Earls
1728	John King	M.A. from Queen's Oxford, Married Henrietta St. Barbe. Gravestone on floor of N. Choir aisle

1742	John Peverel	Divine service twice on Sunday. Communion administered monthly
1780	John Woodburn	Came from York. Minor canon of Salisbury
1807	Daniel Williams	59 years as curate and vicar. Much loved
1833	William Vaux	Canon. Assisted in founding Girls' school
1841	Hon. Gerard Noel	Began restoration of abbey
1851	Walter Carus	Canon. Contributed to building of primary school and adjacent vicarage
1855	Charles Avery Moore	1858 Walker organ installed
1860	Edward Lyon Berthon	See biography on p.128 ff.
1892	James Cooke Yarborough	Gave font in memory of his son, and cross on green in memory of a brother and sister
1910	Hugh M. St.Clair Tapper	
1917	Andrew John Robertson	
1925	William Henry Birch Corban	Canon. Died in harness
1952	Walter Edward Norris	
1971	David Shearlock	Canon. Resigned to become Dean of Truro
1982	Geoffrey Finch	Archdeacon. Died in harness
1984	Neil Crawford-Jones	Appointed hon. canon of Winchester in 1992

APPENDIX THREE

A RE-ASSESSMENT OF KING EDGAR'S CHARTER FOR ROMSEY

Purpose of the Study

A printed copy of this charter is available[1] and an English translation has been made of the second part of the charter which consists of a definition in Anglo Saxon of the abbey boundaries.[2] An interesting LTVAS publication[3] attempts to identify those boundaries on a modern map. The same booklet quotes a few phrases from the lengthy Latin introduction to the charter taken from what is — so far as is known to the present writer the only complete translation which has been made of the — Latin text[4]. One of the quoted phrases refers to 'the renowned convent of the distinguished and secluded community of Romsey'.

My purpose in studying the complete text was to find out what weight could be given to the epithets 'distinguished' and 'secluded' and whether any other details were mentioned about the abbey.

Comparison of the existing translation with the Latin text

On making this comparison, several points became immediately apparent:

1. 'secluded' nowhere appears in the Latin text;

2. a curious phrase, also quoted in the LTVAS booklet, about people who live 'on public roads within the circuit' is also a mistranslation (triviatim by the 10th century no longer meant 'in the public streets' but 'everywhere');

3. there is a whole paragraph about sick persons who are nowhere mentioned in the original, and numerous other errors. It was clearly time for this translation to sink into oblivion!

Authenticity of the charter

Before attempting a fresh translation, I considered the opinions of the experts about the authenticity of the Romsey charter. The earliest extant copy was made several centuries after the date of the original, but nevertheless a number of authorities accept it as authentic[5] Others regard it as 'suspicious' or dismiss it as a forgery[6] because it is one of a group of five charters which share a virtually identical doctrinal preamble in Latin, apart from alteration to the names, places and details peculiar to each abbey.

The other abbeys in the group are Abingdon, Worcester, Muchelney and Pershore. There are, in fact, two charters to Abingdon: one from King Eadred and one from King Edgar who succeeded him. They are the earliest of the group and date from 958/959.

It is reasonable to assume that the person who composed the long theological preface would want to give it the widest possible circulation and he could achieve this by having it read out in a number of different monastic houses. Many such charters were issued and, once a preface had been composed, the scribe had only to copy it and insert the specific details for each abbey.

Even if all five charters were found to be forgeries, this would not affect the composition of the preamble which would have been lifted from a genuine charter. I shall return later to some further reflections on the theology and possible authorship of the preface.

Comparison of the Latin text with other charters of the group

I compared the Romsey text with the similar charter to Abingdon[7] and another to Pershore[8] and found that there were a number of small verbal variations clearly due to errors by the copyist. It was possible by looking for the word or form of word which made best grammatical sense to untangle some, although by no means all, of the obscurities in the Romsey charter.

I found that all the rights and privileges granted to Romsey, including the right to elect their own abbess, are common to all the charters. The epithets 'distinguished' and 'noble' are stock terms, applied to all the abbeys, and nothing individual about Romsey appears until the gifts to the king are recorded at the end of the text.

The gifts of King Edgar in return for the woodland

There is an addition at the end of the Latin section of the Romsey charter which records that, in return for the woodland, the king received a number of valuable gifts from the abbey. The translation often quoted[9] is that he was given 900 mancuses of pure gold in a cup as well as other precious gifts. The convent was wealthy at that period, but even so this would represent a gift of enormous value. Although an ingenious explanation has been offered for this particular sum[10], I believe that a more natural translation of the Latin is that the amount represents the total value of the gifts ('900 mancuses of gold in a goblet of marvellous workmanship, in handsomely chased armlets and in a scabbard richly decorated with gold'). The translation 'to the value of' is supported by Finberg[11]. An additional argument is that it is difficult to conceive of a goblet or vessel large enough to contain 900 gold coins!

There appears to be an interesting confirmation of the gifts in an exceedingly corrupt paragraph in Anglo Saxon at the end of the description of the boundaries. Until recently its interpretation defeated scholars, but a partial reading has been suggested by Dr Ann Williams[12]. She believes that the passage may be a corroboration of the gifts listed above in Latin. Behind the copying errors of a scribe unfamiliar with Anglo Saxon, she picks out apparent descriptions of the (*scabbard*) 'decorated with gold (*gyldene melle*) of which the Latin speaks (*ledene speketh*) and chased armlets (*angrevene beagas*) and the paten (*husel*). (I do not know on what grounds she adds *'given to the convent'*.) The passage is followed by the clear phrase, *'Edmund Atheling lies in the minster'*: this refers to King Edgar's young son who was buried at Romsey in 970/971 AD. (*n.b. Finberg gives 971 x 975 as the date of the Romsey charter*).

Authorship of the preamble and its relevance to the charter's date and authenticity

I turn next to the question of the authorship of the preamble with its long doctrinal statement. Clearly such a preamble, although issued in the name of the king, would not be his own work, nor would it emanate from a mere scribe.

An assessment of Bishop Ethelwold's style and teaching has been made by Michael Lapidge[13]. Details of Ethelwold's education are lacking, but it is known that he became a monk at Glastonbury under Dunstan; that he was later appointed by King Eadred to be abbot of the derelict monastery of Abingdon which he revitalized; and that he was bishop of Winchester from 963 to 984 AD where he worked very closely with King Edgar in the reform of the Church and the imposition of the *Regularis Concordia* as an agreed rule for all English monasteries. Lapidge points to certain idiosyncracies of Ethelwold's style: a fondness for words of Greek origin and some acquaintance with Greek thought, together with an emphasis on orthodoxy expressed in flowery, didactic language.

Lapidge does not directly address himself to the authorship of the preamble, but all the characteristics which he lists are to be found there. Examples of the grecisms are *'basileus'* instead of *'rex'*, *'microcosmus'*, *'hagia'* instead of *'sancta'* etc. His convoluted manner of thought is all too apparent in the translation.

The theology of the preamble

The preface to all five charters begins with an affirmation of orthodoxy, an account of creation (with Adam described as the 'microcosm') and the story of the Fall, with emphasis on the Johannine doctrine of the Logos.

After an anti-Semitic outburst, it condemns the heresies of the Arians and Sabellians. We cannot tell exactly what caused this condemnation, but it looks as though a need to combat heretical teaching lay behind Ethelwold's emphasis on orthodoxy. The Arians believed that God was a being isolated from his creation and that the Son was different in essence from the Father. The Sabellians believed that the historic Christ was a transitory exhibition of God's power and not an essential Person of the Trinity. Both heresies had been condemned at the Council of Nicaea (325 AD) and later General Councils of the Church, but evidently still had their supporters.

Conclusion

The first Abingdon charter claims very clearly to have been drafted by Ethelwold who was at that time its abbot: *Ego Ehelwold abbas hoc eulogium manu propria apicibus depinxi.* In the second Abingdon charter Ethelwold signs it flamboyantly *triumphans dictavi.*

In the Pershore charter, dated 972 and therefore about the same date as the Romsey charter, Ethelwold describes himself as bishop of Winchester and again uses *depinxi* for 'wrote' or 'drafted'. However, above the long list of witnesses a paragraph gives the date of the charter and notes that all the signatories on the list have signed their cross in order of precedence. The word used here for 'signed' is *karaxantur* which Lapidge notes to have been a favourite and idiosyncratic verb of Ethelwold's.

There are no witnesses to the Romsey charter in the extant copy, but if one follows Finberg's conservative line[14] in accepting the charters as genuine, there seems every possibility that the preface was originally drafted by Ethelwold when abbot of Abingdon and that if the signatures had not been lost, the name of the saintly and learned bishop would have been found at the end of the Romsey charter.

TRANSLATION OF THE LATIN INTRODUCTION TO THE ROMSEY CHARTER

We are frequently admonished by the orthodox leaders of the Church that we should serve the people of that town as their vassal for the sake of Christ. He fashioned the fabric of the whole world in a wonderful and ineffable order and at length from the same four-fold matter[15] formed Adam, the microcosm, in the lowest part of the universe. He filled him with the nourishing breath of life in likeness to Himself and provided for him all the delights and pleasures of paradise, with a single exception which was forbidden in order to test him. By his side was placed Eve to be his most fitting companion; but Adam, to his grief, was led astray by the devilish wiles of the crafty serpent and enticed by the scheming of the persuasive woman, without heed of the curse which hung over him. The glutton ate the forbidden apple and was cast out with his posterity for all time into this world of suffering and merited everlasting perdition.

But, as the prophets foretold, a heavenly messenger has brought the tidings for long ages held in secret by the high king of heaven, disclosing the good news from above to those rightly teaching and believing. The message was not as spoken in the outpourings in false and misleading language of the Jews, but striving after the clearest teaching of men of old times and the present, it refutes the Arians and Sabellians and it crushes under foot their foolish allegorical babblings. The messenger vouchsafed that we have been led out of the blindness of deep darkness into the gladness of our heavenly inheritance, now that the gates of heaven have been opened and the gospel truths revealed into the ear of the chaste virgin, who was overwhelmed by the stupendous news.

To her the whole Church cries with loud and united voice, 'Blessed be thou, o Virgin Mary, for thy faith. Those things foretold thee by God shall come to pass.' Wonderful to relate, the Word is incarnate in her body, as recounted by that evangelist who had the highest understanding of universal truth: 'In the beginning was the Word, and the Word was with God and the Word was God' and so forth.

Because the incarnation was brought about through the Virgin, the deception of the first woman is set aside and a shining glory is bestowed on all fruitful women. Therefore by the perfect and redolent divinity of Christ and his own suffering humanity, freedom is mercifully granted to the condemned.

Hence I, Edgar, by divine assistance king of the English and of the other peoples dwelling anywhere in the surrounding lands, in order that I may be found worthy to have part in the fellowship of the community by the mercy of the High King who is the source of this freedom, do concede for ever the liberty of monastic privilege to the religious community in the well-known place which is called by its inhabitants of ancient stock by the noble name of Romsey, a site which is dedicated to the holy Mother of our Lord Jesus Christ.

The liberty of this privilege shall be held successively in perpetual use by the nuns, living under rule, after the death of the renowned abbess Merwenna, in whose time the restoration of this privilege has been granted, as Christ is my witness, so long as the whole congregation of the aforesaid community shall elect their abbess in council, according to the Rule instituted by the order of the blessed Benedict, and shall choose her justly from the same company of sisters. Let no outsider, exercising tyrannical and obstinate disobedience in the aforesaid convent, seize the right of power, but let the congregation of this same community glory in the privilege of this perpetual liberty which I have proclaimed.

Moreover, let the aforesaid convent be free from all yoke of earthly service in the same manner in which it was held by ancient privilege from the catholic kings, our predecessors. By this decree IT IS ABSOLVED. Equally, those lands which have been conceded out of clemency to the use of the nuns, both in ancient and modern times, by kings and religious persons of both sexes and by me myself, out of divine respect for our Lord Jesus Christ and his mother Mary, are to have their rights restored in order that they may enjoy the same liberty in perpetuity.

If, however, anyone, led astray by maniacs with insane greed for gain, should try against our wishes to violate our generous gift by rash audacity, let him be expelled from the fellowship of God's holy Church, and from participation in the sacred body and blood of Jesus Christ, the son of God, through whom the whole world is freed from the ancient enemy of our race. With Judas the betrayer of Christ, he is consigned to Christ's left hand16 unless he shall first humbly repent and make worthy amends. Because he has presumed to act as a rebel against God's holy Church: let him neither obtain pardon in an active life nor being a renegade find peace in the cloister, but thrust into the eternal fires of hell with Ananias and Sapphira, let the wretched man suffer eternal torments.

For the woodland pertaining to this demesne gifts were given to the said king of a goblet of marvellous workmanship, handsomely chased armlets and a scabbard richly decorated with gold, together worth 900 mancuses of pure gold.

REFERENCES

1. W.de Gray Birch, *Cartularium Saxonicum* no.1187
2. G.B.Grundy, *Archæological Journal* Vol.84, 1927
3. Lower Test Valley Archæological Society (LTVAS), *When the Nuns Ruled Romsey*, 1978
4. Edmund Parsons, *Hampshire Chronicle*, 23rd July 1921
5. H.P.R.Finberg, *The Early Charters of Wessex*, pp.19,58 & Eric John, *Orbis Britanniae*, 1966
6. D.Whitelock, *English Historical Documents*, Vol.i & Simon Keynes, *Diplomas of King Æthelred*, p.98 7.Birch, op.cit. no.1047
8. Birch, op.cit. no.1282
9. E.g. LTVAS op.cit., H.Liveing, *Records of Romsey Abbey*
10. Christopher Collier, *Hampshire Field Club*, Vol.46, 1990
11. Finberg, op.cit. no.123
12. Ed.J.H.Stevenson, Wilts Record Society no.45, 1987
13. ed.B.Yorke, *Bishop Æthelwold*, Chap. Four, 1987, and ed.M.Lapidge, *Wulfstan of Winchester's Life of St. Æthelwold*, 1991, introd. p.lxxxix
14. Finberg, op.cit., Introduction
15. i.e. earth, air, fire and water
16. Matth.25.32

APPENDIX FOUR

THE TWO HISTORIATED CAPITALS

The interpretation of the two historiated capitals facing outwards on the easternmost pillars of the north and south choir aisles.

It is impossible to reach a final conclusion about the significance of these two scenes, but some previous hypotheses may be ruled out and certain pointers are worth noting.

The first mistake is to dismiss the capitals as unimportant because they are tucked away in the farthest corners of the church. On the contrary, as we have seen on page 16, they would have occupied important symbolic positions on the nuns' processional route. Historiated capitals often relate Biblical stories, but here the scenes appear to be connected with the foundation of the nunnery and the dedication of the church.

On the north capital is the gory battle scene shown above. Heads are decapitated, large birds fly off with human carrion and a riderless horse flees from the field of battle. In the centre there are two kings. Their swords are held back by angels to prevent further violence and one king appears to be touching or pulling the other's beard. Possibly the scene is intended to depict the Battle of Ethandune (Edington)[1] in Wiltshire between King Alfred and Guthrum the Danish king in the year 878. Guthrum was defeated but not killed and by the subsequent Treaty of Wedmore the kingdom of Wessex was freed from Danish rule and Guthrum accepted Christian baptism with Alfred as his sponsor[2]. The peaceful settlement may have opened the way for the founding (or re-founding) of this religious house. It is difficult to find any other explanation for this scene.

In 968 AD King Edgar granted to the abbey lands at Edington and Ashton in Wiltshire. The grant included the area where the Battle of Edington had been fought which Alfred had bequeathed to his wife Ealhswith in his will. Just as he granted her for her lifetime the land in Winchester on which Nunnaminster was later built, possibly at his express wish, he might have had a similar intention for the nunnery at Romsey, even though no record survives.

Some commentators have described the touching of the beard as an act of submission -- in which case it would be made by Guthrum -- but it is doubtful whether it has any special significance. Examples of beard-pulling are to be found on French romanesque capitals and are said to have their origin in Islamic art[3]. They represent 'discord' and are normally balanced (e.g. at Poitiers) by another scene of two embracing figures who represent 'concord'. The mason at Romsey may have been familiar with the Poitiers carving and thought that the beard-pulling suited his purpose.

When a sculptor was given a theme, as here, it seems to have been common practice to leave him free in the execution of it to follow popular taste or a known exemplar or his own idiosyncracies[4]. Such freedom appears to have been the case in this instance and is a more acceptable explanation than that of the 19th century writer who alleged that Alfred by touching Guthrum's beard was promising to become his godfather - an explanation which seems to have more to do with leg-pulling than beard-pulling[5].

If the north capital relates to the Saxon foundation of the abbey, one might expect the one on the opposite side to relate to the dedication of the present Norman church. Three separate scenes appear to be depicted. On the left face, a seated king and standing angel hold a V-shaped scroll which reads ROBERxT mE fecit (sic) i.e. *Robert made me*. In the centre another crowned figure holds a pyramid or obelisk, presumably representing the church and referring to its royal foundation. On the right are two seated figures in cloaks and cloth caps who may be masons. They hold another scroll with a more cryptic Latin inscription: RobERT TUTE CONSULe x d s (sic). There is no obvious explanation for the final symbols which remain a mystery. Above this scroll, on the corner of the capital, is a grotesque, but cheerful, grinning face. If the inscription is in Latin, it is obscure. The phrase has been construed as *Robert, look around you* (i.e. at your handiwork), or as *Robert, take very great care*, but neither translation is convincing.

Partly for this reason and partly because it is often mistakenly asserted that masons never signed their handiwork (see below), Robert has sometimes been identified with Robert Earl of Gloucester (sometimes referred to as 'consul' of Gloucester). He was Henry I's natural son and a wealthy patron of art. For this explanation to stand, the 'e' has to be dropped off consule and added to the last three unexplained symbols. Earl Robert has no known connection with Romsey; he opposed King Stephen in the civil war and it is strange for him to be associated with this church where Stephen's daughter was abbess.

It is unlikely that this great church was the gift of a single donor and Dr.John H.Harvey[6] asserts positively that *me fecit* must apply to the sculptor: to describe a donor or patron *fieri fecit* (*caused to be made*) would be used. Benefactions could be expected for a nunnery with so many royal connections, and Christina, the future Queen Matilda and Mary de Blois may each in her time have brought an influx of wealth, but the pauses in the building programme which spread the work out over more than a century indicate that the necessary finance had to be raised in stages.

It was common for a religious house to have the equivalent of a modern 'fabric fund' built up from various sources: specific revenues might be allotted to it, special appeals and collections organized, requests made for legacies and indulgences offered. It is therefore difficult to see how any one individual could claim credit for the whole building.

The crowned figures might have been present at a ceremony of dedication as patrons rather than donors. It has been pointed out[7] that the two kings on the northern capital are bearded, whereas the standing king on the south capital has a square, clean-shaven chin, apparently to indicate that he is a different character. Normans tended to be clean-shaven and Saxons to be bearded.

To return to the inscriptions, another explanation is that the right-hand Robert was an office-holder or warden of the masons' lodge. It is possible that the two seated masons (i.e. the carvers) are having a joke at the expense of their boss, or else that one of the two masons (who carved the grotesque face) is labelling the other (who carved the main scenes). Simon Owers points out that the sculptor of this face also carved the 'smiling lions' (central capital of the retrochoir). The faces are similar and there is the same curious 'horned band' above the heads. On the other hand, the rest of this capital was certainly carved by the same mason as the one who carved the battle scene. The treatment of the figures is similar: neat and careful, but somewhat flat. Owers also remarks that the seated masons on the south capital are similar to the seated figure warming his hands by the fire in the 'February' scene on the north side of St.Ethelfleda's chapel, but he thinks that for artistic reasons this capital and the 'smiling lions' capital were not by the same hand.

Artistically, his argument is convincing, but he fails to draw out the inevitable consequence: namely, that two different hands must have been at work on the southern historiated capital. For simplicity's sake I refer to them as the 'serious' mason who carved all the detailed scenes, and the 'jester' mason who carved the grotesque face. This approaches Dr. Harvey's view that there were two different Roberts at Romsey: the carver who made the work; and Robert (?Tute) who was 'consul', either as a donor or an office-holder. Nevertheless Dr.Harvey is convinced that the inscription can apply only to the carvings and not to the whole church. The present writer believes that the 'serious' or senior carver depicted the two scenes which alone among the capitals describe historical events connected with Romsey Abbey and were therefore not to be left to the whims of the band of carvers responsible for the other capitals and who, as we have seen from Chapter Two, took their themes from other sources. Once the historical scene was completed, the 'jester' Robert could take over.

Dr. Harvey quotes a number of instances of masons' signatures from the Norman period in England[8] and there are even more examples to be found in France. At Autun *Gislebertus me fecit* is prominently displayed under the Last Judgement scene on the tympanum. At Clermont-Ferrand a Master Robert was the carver of four historiated capitals in the apse of the basilica of Notre-Dame-du-Port and signed one of them[9]. Both these sculptures are from approximately the same date as those at Romsey.

In the past the view was sometimes expressed that masons would not sign their work because they occupied a humble position in society and were paid as journeymen on the same basis as carpenters and other workmen. The free masons, however, were very different men from the rough-masons and they later formed themselves into powerful guilds. A skilled master mason

a. N. choir aisle: seated figures and smiling face

b. Retrochoir: smiling lion

c. St. Ethelfleda's chapel: seated figures in 'February' scene

was much sought after by would-be employers. If the masons were practising architects, they were treated with great respect. Harvey[10] quotes a letter from the master mason at Calais written to King Henry V: while the writer apologizes for his 'rude and uncunning writing', the king had evidently encouraged him to correspond direct and report his progress. There is also a handsome tombstone of a mason at East Winch in Norfolk, identified by the tools of his trade, which shows that he must have prospered in his career.

At present the interpretation of the two historiated capitals in Romsey Abbey remains an open question, but previous views and some tentative suggestions to take the argument a little further have been set out at some length in the hope that an expert will be stimulated to make a fresh examination of the subject.

NOTES AND REFERENCES

1. The identification of Ethandune with Edington is generally accepted.
2. ASC (Laud version).
3. Simon Owers, unpublished dissertation on Romsey capitals quoting Zehava Jacoby, *Art Medieval II,ii*
4. Coulton, Art & Ref, p.250.
5. Royal Soc. of Antiquaries, XXVIII, p.304, W.Latham.
6. Harvey, private correspondence and *English Medieval Architects*, revised 1984, p.255.
7. Simon Owers, op.cit.
8. Harvey, *Eng.Med.Architects*, 1984 ed. pp.5,115,151,253.
9. I am indebted to Mrs T.Grimwood for this information.
10. Harvey, *The Med. Architect*, pp.88-89.

APPENDIX FIVE

MARY DE BLOIS

Dates and Charters relating to the move of Mary de Blois from Lillechurch and her election as Abbess of Romsey

There is a collection of recorded charters signed by Henry II in England and witnessed by Thomas Becket while chancellor. Although undated, these must have been issued between 1155 (when Thomas was appointed chancellor) and 1158 when Henry left England for France.

One of these charters was issued at Canterbury and confirms the manor of Lillechurch to Mary. After her mother's death, the lordship of that manor was inherited by her elder brother Eustace, but he died in 1153 and it then passed to her younger brother, William. He confirmed the gift of this land to his sister Mary in accordance with his parents' wishes. In the grant he asks for the prayers of the nuns for his soul and for the souls of so many of his family who had died before him.[1] It is the validity of this grant which is confirmed in Henry II's charter.[2]

The first occasion on which Henry II visited Canterbury as king and could have issued charters from there was on 1st January 1156. The following day he moved on to Dover and issued some more charters.[3] One of these was to St.Mary's Abbey, Leicester, and the witnesses included Thomas the Chancellor, Earl Reginald (of Cornwall) and Richard de Lucy (the justiciar). These same witnesses also signed the charter which confirmed Lillechurch to Mary. They were evidently part of the king's entourage at that time and would have been at Canterbury with him on the previous day.

We may take it therefore that Mary was still at Lillechurch Priory in January 1156. However, some time before leaving England in 1158, Henry issued several charters to Romsey Abbey, including one from Salisbury in February or March 1158.[4] One at least is personally addressed to *Marie Filie regis Stephani et monialibus suis*.[5] It can therefore be stated with some confidence that Mary moved to Romsey some time between spring 1156 and spring 1158.

The second question is the reason for her move. Her position at Lillechurch as nominal prioress of a small group of French nuns, who had already caused conflict in their previous convent, was probably unsatisfactory, but the main reason most likely lay in the need of Romsey Abbey for further patronage. The nuns were in the middle of building the great new church, begun c.1120 but still unfinished. Patronage usually depended on having an abbess of noble or royal birth. The previous abbess died in 1155. There was usually something of a gap between elections while formalities were concluded, but the probability is that the royal princess, Mary de Blois, was asked for and elected during the year 1156.

REFERENCES

1.   Dugdale, vol.IV, p.382
2.   *Recueil*, vol.I, p.143, no.xlii
3.   Eyton, p.15
4.   Ib. p.35
5.   *Recueil*, vol. I, p.144

APPENDIX SIX

THE PROVENANCE OF THE FIFTEENTH CENTURY PSALTER

The psalter was examined by the Rev. F.W.H. Davy after its purchase from the antiquarian booksellers, Quaritch & Co. in 1900. His very full description may be found in Liveing's *Records of Romsey Abbey*, pages 285-297. The purpose of this appendix is merely to explain the reasons for the conclusion of experts, as quoted in Chapter Four, that the psalter was written in England, apparently for Franciscan use, in the vicinity of Romsey, but belonged by the sixteenth century to the Benedictine nuns of Winchester.

The style of hand-writing reveals that the psalter was written in England. The calendar at the beginning of the book is significant in that the feasts of St.Francis and St.Ethelfleda are given in red. However, there are twenty-six marginal additions in one hand, belonging to the sixteenth century, which connect the book from that date to St.Mary's Abbey, Winchester, because they give the obits of seven close relatives of St.Edburga, its patron saint, (including those of her grandparents, King Alfred and Queen Ealhswith) as well as of eighteen Winchester abbesses. Undoubtedly, therefore, by the sixteenth century ownership of the psalter had passed into the hands of St.Mary's Abbey.

The calendar is followed by a liturgical psalter, six ferial canticles and a litany. In the litany it is noteworthy that the name of Francis immediately follows that of Benedict, and St.Clare is invoked in the place of the usual St.Anastasia. There is no provision for saints' day services and the psalter seems to have been intended for private devotional use rather than as an office book.

Davy suggests that the book might originally have been written by or for a Franciscan friar who acted as confessor to some of the Romsey nuns. This would explain the inclusion of the feasts of St.Ethelfleda, even though the psalter was never actually owned by Romsey Abbey.

The name of St.Thomas of Canterbury and of the pope's title 'pape' have been erased, as ordered by King Henry VIII, but what happened to the psalter between the dissolution and the time when it turned up in the sale-room is unknown. The name of T.H.Lloyd appears on the fly-leaf in modern writing and the psalter was re-bound in the nineteenth century.

APPENDIX SEVEN

THOMAS WARREN'S TOMBSTONE

Explanation of alternative years of death found on tombstones of Thomas Warren and several other people buried in the abbey in the 17th and early 18th centuries

According to the reckoning of the time in England Thomas Warren died in 1693, so what considerations led his executors to put 1693/4 on his tombstone? The starting-point in our investigation is the change from the Julian to the Gregorian calendar, which took place in European countries between the 16th and 18th centuries, with a change in new year's day from March 25th to January 1st. Two entirely different repercussions of these changes were the popular cry of 'Give us back our eleven days' when England adopted the Gregorian calendar; and the date we still use for the end of the tax year - April 5th.

Why and how did these changes take place? The Julian calendar, introduced in 46 BC, made the year eleven and a quarter minutes too long. In 1581 Pope Gregory XIII issued an edict annulling 10 days and making 5th October 1582 into 15th October; and, to prevent the error recurring, he ordained that century years should not be leap years until they were divisible by 400. He also made January 1st into new year's day instead of March 25th, the Feast of the Annunciation known as Lady Day. The Gregorian calendar was adopted at once in Roman Catholic countries, but Protestant ones were mostly slow in following suit. Scotland made the change in 1600, the Protestant states of Germany about 1700 and, when England finally took the plunge in 1752, all the Protestant countries on the continent had already fallen into line.

The changes were made in England in the following way. The year 1751 was shortened by nearly three months, to allow 1752 to begin on January 1st. Then the error in the Julian calendar, now eleven days, was corrected by making the day after 2nd September 1752 into 14th September. It was this jump in the calendar which prompted the cry 'Give us back our eleven days': many people thought that they were being cheated out of eleven days of their lives and out of eleven days' pay. At the same time, no one in authority dared to take eleven days off the fiscal year, which is why our tax year now ends on April 5th instead of on Lady Day.

Against the background of a gradual acceptance of the Gregorian calendar throughout Europe, to avoid misunderstandings people in England in the 17th and first half of the 18th centuries, if they had contacts with Scotland or the continent, sometimes in their correspondence gave a double year-date for days between 1st January and 24th March. Similarly, on tombstones there might be a desire to avoid uncertainty later on about the year in which a person with contacts abroad had actually died. In the years of religious intolerance, many reformists took refuge in Holland where complete freedom of worship prevailed. Thomas Warren may well have had friends there.

APPENDIX EIGHT

JOHN KENT MEMORIAL

Joannis Kent Armigeri
olim de civitate Londinensi Silkethrower
hujusce postea Oppidi bis Praetoris,
et comitatus Southtoniae nuper
Vicecomitis:
Viri
eximia erga Deum pietate
erga suos benignitate et amore
erga alios probitate et humanitate
erga pauperes (tam currente vita
quam exacta) beneficentia,
apprime illustris et spectabilis.
Obiit 2do die Novembris Anno Dni 1692
Annoque aetatis 70mo
Quicum una requiescit Juditha uxor
Charissima simul atque amantissima;
quae decessit e vita 15 Die Novembris 1674
Annoque aetatis 63.
Utrique hoc monumentum posuere
Gratitudinis et pietatis ergo
Thomas Shory, Ioannes Butler et
Thomas Butler Praedicto Ioanni Kent
Multis nominibus devinctissimi
Supremi Testamenti
CURATORES

TRANSLATION

This memorial has been placed by his friends in honour of John Kent Esquire, at one time silk-thrower of the City of London, later twice mayor of this town, and in recent times Sheriff of the County of Southampton; a man particularly distinguished and remarkable for his singular piety towards God, goodwill and love towards his friends, justice and humanity towards others and generosity towards the poor (both during his lifetime and after his death). He died on November 2nd 1692 AD at the age of 70.

Together with him rests his wife Judith, greatly loved and greatly loving, who departed this life November 15th 1674 at the age of 63.

To both of these, in gratitude and piety, this memorial has been set up by Thomas Shory, John Butler and Thomas Butler, who are deeply indebted on many counts to the aforesaid John Kent, and trustees of his last will and testament.

APPENDIX NINE

THE ORGAN APPEAL FOR £200,000 LAUNCHED IN 1992

Technical details of repairs required (supplied by Jeffrey Williams, Romsey Abbey Organist)

In 1858 J.W.Walker & Sons built a three manual and pedal organ of 33 speaking stops in the north transept gallery of the abbey. When in 1888 as a result of the re-ordering of the fabric of the abbey the organ was moved to its present position in the chancel, Walker again carried out the work and added four new speaking stops and a tremulant. The new layout of the various departments of the organ meant that a variety of actions had to be installed to enable the player to control the instrument and, in all, three different actions were used: the Swell on tubular pneumatic, the Pedal on pneumatic and tracker (both departments are sited in the triforium) the Great on Barker Lever and the Choir retaining its 1858 tracker action.

The organ remained in the care of Walker until just after the First World War when it was given to Ivimey and Cooper of Southampton. In 1954 Willis bought Ivimey and Cooper and the organ then passed into their care. After the 1888 work the organ received little attention other than routine tuning and maintenance (though in 1960 Walker were asked to draw up a major rebuilding scheme which included electrification of the action and the provision of a new console with sweeping changes to the stop list but this never came to fruition). It was not until 1974, almost ninety years later that the organ was to receive any major attention. Once more the work was given to Walker and in addition to a general overhaul and cleaning the schedule included the repalletting of the soundboards, releathering the swell reservoir, addition of a balanced swell pedal, revoicing of the reeds and re-covering of the keys, none of the actions was to be rebuilt or replaced. The final invoice for the work was £15,250 plus £680 for a humidifier which was installed at the same time.

By 1981 the shortcomings and defects of the actions installed in 1888 had become very apparent, particularly the pneumatic actions in the triforium. A decision was taken to get N.P.Mander to try to improve the situation but yet again no replacing or rebuilding of any of the action was undertaken. The wind pressure to the Barker Lever was increased which improved its effectiveness but inevitably resulted in greatly increased action noise and much heavier touch. The swell penumatic action was regulated and fine tuned. The rest of the work involved the restoring of the Great sharp mixture to its 1888 pitch of 26.29 and the Great four foot harmonic flute to a twelfth as it was in the original 1858 specification. It was at this time too that the splendid Tuba was added.

Unfortunately the 1981 work on the action resulted in only a short term improvement and over the past eleven years the situation has deteriorated, gradually at first but the deterioration has accelerated quite alarmingly over the past two years.

The pipework of the abbey organ is without doubt some of the best of its kind to be found. The organ stands as a testament to the work of the J.W.Walker and is a superb example of an English Victorian organ which remains largely untouched from its 1858 specification. The problem is still with the action and it is only a matter to time before the situation gets so bad as to make the organ unplayable and unable to do its job. Because of its considerable historical importance and the quality of the pipework it is essential that the organ is preserved to lead and inspire the worship at the abbey in the next century. A scheme of work has been drawn up by J.W.Walker which involves replacing the clumsy and worn out 1888 pneumatic action in the triforium with a modern mechanical one. The Barker Lever action to the Great will be retained but completely stripped, restored and reset. The tracker action of the Choir which is as responsive today as it probably was in 1858 needs only minor attention. At the same time as this work is being done the opportunity will be taken to add some discrete but very necessary playing aids to the console in order to make the organist's job a little easier than it is at present. No alterations will be made to the instrument's tonal specification. This scheme is the only real long-term solution to a problem which has plagued us for so long. It is one which preserves the historical parts of the organ which are worth saving but replaces those which are not and equips the organ for its role in the abbey into the next century.

At the same time as this work is undertaken (or at a later date if the funds are not available) a few ranks of pipes could be placed discretely in one of the nave triforium bays and could be played from the main organ so that the congregation would have a much better lead in their singing than the organ gives at present. This nave section could also be equipped with its own mobile console so that if the main organ were not needed (for example, at the monthly Family Eucharist) the nave organ could be played. It would also be possible for the main organ to be played from the nave console which would give even greater flexibility so that at services when the choir was not present the organist could be much nearer to the congregation and feel much more a part of the service than he does now.

SUMMARY OF REQUIRED EXPENDITURE

For restoration:

    £40,000   to clean and overhaul entire organ

    £15,000   to replace old pneumatic Swell action with new mechanical action

    £19,000   to revise and rebuild the clumsy Pedal action

For playing aids:

    £17,000   to rebuild and redesign the stop action

    £ 5,000   to provide 10 combination pedals

          £97,000   TOTAL

For a nave section:

    £35,000 to provide a small seven stop Nave Organ playable from the Main Organ

    £ 9,500 to install a single manual and pedal console in the nave to operate the small organ only, or

    £13,000 to install a Nave Console from which both organs can be played

£145,000 GRAND TOTAL

Allowing for inflation and other eventualities the appeal aims at £200,000.

APPENDIX TEN

TWENTIETH CENTURY GIFTS AND ACQUISITIONS

It would be impossible to itemize all the gifts which have been made to the church over the last century, but even the smallest have maintained a quality of workmanship worthy of this great building. Mention of three items must suffice.

Fifteenth century carved walnut chest (in north aisle)

This chest was a generous gift to the abbey early this century from Mr. C. H. Sloane Stanley. It was analyzed in a monograph published by the Furniture History Society[1] and described as workmanship of the very highest quality. It was probably made in northern France. The flamboyant tracery panels of the front and sides of the chest are elaborately and expertly carved. There is a vertical panel down the centre front for the lock plate, below which there is a carved shield *chevronée*, surmounted by a coronet. The writer comments on how well the pierced tracery of the lock plate and the small Christ figure on the hasp are integrated into the whole design: woodworker and smith have each contributed their craft in a perfect alliance to achieve a piece of furniture of outstanding quality.

Bas-relief of Madonna and Child (above the high altar): see front cover illustration

This bas-relief which creates a focal point above the altar is the work of Martin Travers (1886-1948) who was a noted stained glass artist and ecclesiastical designer between the wars. He was a pupil of Sir Ninian Comper (1864-1960) who was himself described as a Kempe-trained glazier and church designer. A very similar bas-relief by Travers is in Beaulieu church.

Statue of the Annunciation (St. Anne's Chapel)

This sculpture, donated in 1974 in memory of Edith and Stanley Vane, is of the Virgin Mary. There is no need to see the angel or hear Mary's response of *Be it unto me according to your word*. Her bearing and expression of calm acceptance convey her reply to the angel's message. The carving is the work of a distinguished sculptor, Michael Clark, who died in 1987. As a devout Catholic, he carried out many commissions for churches and cathedrals, including an outstanding sculpture of 'Our Lady of the Assumption' at Aylesford, Kent. He was awarded the silver medal of the Royal Society of Sculptors in 1967 for his carved relief of the welcoming Christ over the west door of Westminster Abbey, and was President of the Society from 1971 to 1976.

REFERENCE

1.   P. Eames, 'Furniture in England, France and the Netherlands from the Twelfth to the Fifteenth Century' under the cover title of *Medieval Furniture*, London 1977.

EXAMPLES OF ARCHITECTURAL STYLES TO BE FOUND IN THE ABBEY

1. Early English (c.1250) abutting Norman (c.1150) arches, west end of nave

2. East window of choir, Decorated style (c.1300)

3. Perpendicular style (c.1400) in north nave wall

BIBLIOGRAPHY

Addleshaw, G. and **Etchells, F.**, *The Architectural Setting of Anglican Worship* (Faber 1948)

Andrewes, Lancelot, *Ninety-six Sermons*, (Oxford 1841)

Anglo-Saxon Chronicle

Archer, Michael, *Stained Glass* (Pitkin Pictorials 1979)

Balleine, G.R., *The Layman's History of the Church of England* (1923)

Berthon, E.W., *A Retrospect of Eight Decades*, (George Bell & Sons 1899)

Birch, W. de Gray, *Cartularium Saxonicum vol.3; Liber de Hyda* (1892)

Blair, Peter Hunter, *Introduction to Anglo Saxon England* (Cambridge, 2nd edition 1977)

Bouquet (ed.), *Ex Actis Thomae, Arch. Cant.*

Calendar of Close Rolls, Henry III

Capes, W.W., *Bishops of Winchester. pt.II 'Walkelin to Gardiner'* (1907) Reprinted from the "Winchester Diocesan Chronicle"

Chartres et Diplomes relatifs a l'histoire de France, Recueil des Actes de Henri II

Coatsworth, E., 'Late pre-Conquest Sculptures', *Bishop Æthelwold*, ed. B. Yorke (Boydell 1988)

Coldicott, D.K., *Hampshire Nunneries* (Phillimore 1989)

Collett, Barry, 'Richard Fox' in *Monastic Studies* (Headstart History 1990)

Collier, Christopher, 'Romsey Minster in Saxon Times', *Proceedings of the Hampshire Field Club*, vol.46 (1990)

Cook, G.H., *English Monasteries in the Middle Ages* (Phoenix House 1961)

Coulton, G.G., *Medieval Panorama* (Cambridge 1949); *Art and the Reformation* (Cambridge, 1928)

Cowen, Painton, *A Guide to Stained Glass in Britain*, (Michael Joseph 1985)

Cressy, David, *Education in Tudor and Stuart England* (E. Arnold 1975)

Crossley, F.H., *The English Abbey* (Batsford 1935)

Dale, P.G. *Sir W.P. of Romsey*, (LTVAS Group 1987)

Dugdale, William, *Monasticon Anglicanum*

Eames, Penelope, *Medieval Furniture* (Furniture History Society, London 1977)

Eyton, R.W., *Itinerary of King Henry II* (James Foster, Dorchester 1878)

Finberg, H., *The Early Charters of Wessex* (Leicester 1964)

Genge P. and **Spinney J.,** *Romsey Schools: 900 until 1940* (LTVAS Publication 1991)

The Gentleman's Magazine, vol.xiv, new series, August 1840

Godwin, G.N., *The Civil War in Hampshire* (Laurence Oxley, Alresford, republished 1973)

Green, A.R., 'The Romsey Painted Wooden Reredos', *Archaeological Journal*, vol.xc

Green, M.Everett, *Princesses of England*, vol.i (Miss Wood)

Grout, D.J., *A History of Western Music* (Dent, 2nd edition 1973)

Grundy, M.A., 'The Saxon Land Charters of Hampshire', *Archaeological Journal*, vol.84

Harvey, John H., *The Medieval Architect* (Wayland 1972); *English Medieval Architects* (Alan Sutton, revised edn. 1987)

Hearn, M.F., '*Romsey Abbey: A Progenitor of the English National Tradition in Architecture'*, Gesta 1975

Hibbert, C., *The English, A Social History 1066-1945* (Paladin 1988)

Jacoby, Zehava, The Beard Pullers in Islamic Art: an Islamic Motif and its Evolution in the West', *Art Medieval*, II,ii

John, Eric, *Orbis Britanniae* (Leicester 1966)

Ker, N.R. and **Piper, A.J.**, *Medieval Manuscripts in British Libraries* (Clarendon Press 1992)

Knowles, D., Brooke, C. and **London, V.**, *The Heads of Religious Houses England and Wales* (Cambridge 1972)

Lapidge, M. and **Winterbottom, M.** (eds.), *Wulfstan of Winchester's Life of St. Æthelwold* (Oxford 1991)

Liveing, H., *Records of Romsey Abbey 907-1558* (Warren & Son, Winchester 1906)

Luce, R., *Pages from the History of Romsey and its Abbey* (Warren & Son, Winchester 1948)

McCann, Justin, *The Rule of St. Benedict* (Sheed & Ward, transl.1976)

Moorman, J.R.H., *A History of the Church in England* (A. & C. Black 1980)

Paul, John, 'Hampshire Recusants in time of Elizabeth I', *Proceedings of the Hampshire Field Club*, vol.xxi, pt.2 (1959)

Pevsner, N. and **Lloyd, D.**, *Hampshire and the Isle of Wight* (Penguin Books 1967)

Power, E., *Medieval English Nunneries* (Cambridge 1922)

Saltman, A., *Theobald, Archbishop of Canterbury* (London, Athlone Press 1956)

Sawyer, P., *Anglo-Saxon Charters* (Royal Historical Society 1968)

Scott, I.R. *et al.*, (forthcoming) *Monograph on Romsey Abbey*, TVAT (sponsored by English Heritage)

Spence, C., *An Essay descriptive of the Abbey Church of Romsey* 2nd ed. also entitled *Handbook to Romsey Abbey* (Lordan, Romsey 1841)

Strauss, E., *Sir William Petty, Portrait of a Genius*

Styan, K.E., *Sepulchral Cross Slabs* (Bemrose & Sons, London 1902)

Thompson, A.H., *English Monasteries* (Cambridge 1913)

Tristram, E.W., *English Medieval Wall Paintings* (Oxford 1950)

Urquhart, M., *Sir John St.Barbe Bt. of Broadlands* (Paul Cave, Southampton 1983)

Walker, F.G., *A Short History of Romsey* (Miss Chignell, Romsey 1896)

Yorke, B. (ed.), *Bishop Æthelwold, His Career and Influence*, (Boydell 1988)

Zettl, E., *An Anonymous Short English Metrical Chronicle* (Early English Text Society 1935)

MANUSCRIPT SOURCES AND UNPUBLISHED DISSERTATION

Latham, John, *Collections for a History of Romsey* (BL 26774-26780); Typescript held by LTVAS, Romsey
Owers, Simon, *The carved capitals of Romsey Abbey* (unpublished dissertation)
Spence, C. *Manuscript Notes*

Carved heads and moulding from the tower (p.45)

PLAN OF ROMSEY ABBEY

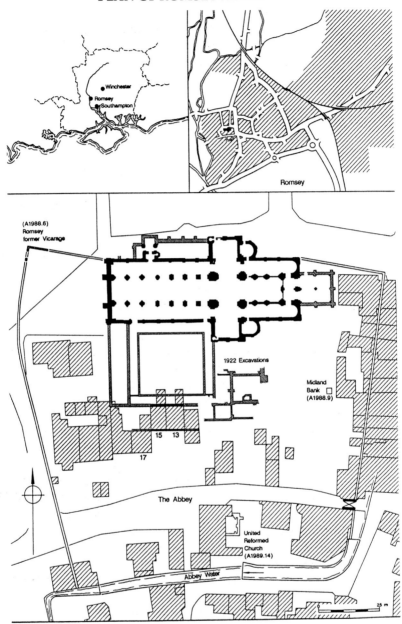

Location of Abbey, Abbey Precinct and Minor Excavations within the Precinct

ILLUSTRATIONS

Every effort has been made to acknowledge sources and contact owners of copyright. I apologize for any oversight. Cattermole, Buckler and Mallows illustrations are from a collection in the vicarage.

Front cover

Saxon rood by permission of English Life Publications Ltd, other photographs by S. Sales, design by R. Emuss.

5	Abbey seal of St.Ethelfleda, 1813 drawing by B. Howlett
7	Plaited hair, from *Gentleman's magazine* 1840
9	Norman doorway and Saxon rood, early 20th century post card
12	Church from south-east in 1895, drawn by C. E. Mallows
17	Drawings of capitals by D. Hargreaves
17/18	Historiated capitals from *Archaeologia* 23.4.1802, by permission of Society of Antiquaries
19	N.E. view of chancel, drawn by R. Cattermole c.1820
20	Norman arcading round tower crossing, photograph by C. T. Drew
21	S. transept c.1895, drawn by C. E. Mallows
22	South side of nave, photograph by C. T. Drew
25	South side of nave with giant column, drawn by G. Cattermole
26	East windows of choir
27	Norman doorway, photograph by S. Sales
29	*Sheila-na-gig,,* drawn by M. Howard
30	Flamboyant Perpendicular window, drawn by J. Wills
31	Mouldings (a. and d.) by permission of HFC, vol.II, pp.9 & 11
36	Part of s. transept, drawn by R. Cattermole
37	St. Scholastica & St. Benedict, photograph by M. Howard
41	Four heads from wooden screen, photograph by S. Sales
42	Effigy, drawn by Burkitt, Brit. Archaeological Congress 1844
43	Tombstones of abbesses, drawings by Burkitt and Carter
45	King's head, drawn from photograph
47	Medieval paving tile, supplied by TVAT
68	A Benedictine abbess, unascribed
75	Church interior 1865, by permission of Illustrated London News Picture Library
77	West end and font, drawn by R. Cattermole

78   Chancel drawn by Latham, by permission of BL, Add.26775
81   N. front of church c.1820, drawn by J. Buckler
83   Chancel restored by Berthon c.1895, by C. E. Mallows
89   St. Barbe monument, photograph by C. T. Drew
91   Earl Mountbatten of Burma, photograph by C. T. Drew
97   Corbel of fiddler, from parish magazine, Sept. 1980
99   Coster organ in 1838, drawn by G. F. Sergeant
102   Walker organ in chancel, photograph by C. T. Drew
104   Stairs to ringing chamber, photograph by C. T. Drew
106   The abbey bells, photograph by C. T. Drew
110   The bell chamber, photograph by C. T. Drew
112   Sketch of Rouen window reproduced in *Bulletin des amis des monuments Rouennais, 1976/7*
115   Detail from Romsey panel
124   Heads in s. transept, drawn by M. Howard
128   Rev. E. L. Berthon, from autobiography, with consent of surviving members of Berthon family
134   Chancel (as on p.78)
136   Pavilion erected by Berthon
143   Abbey from the Test, 1777, by permission of BL, Add.26775
xii-xiii Capitals, as on pp.17-18
xv   a. from photograph by C. T. Drew
        b. from photograph by C. T. Drew
        c. from photograph by F. Houlston

Architectural Styles

xxvi   1. Norman and Early English bays, drawn by G. D. Carter
        2. Decorated window, drawn by J. L. Petit
        3. Perpendicular windows, drawn by J. Wills
xxix   Carved heads from tower, drawn by M. Howard
xxx   Plan of Romsey Abbey, by permission of TVAT

Index of Proper Names

Abingdon   vii, viii
Act for Burying in Wool   141
Act of Uniformity   74
Adam, Robert   86
Adderley, John   108
Aelfric, Archbishop   10
Albert, Prince Consort   41, 131
Alfred, the Great   1, 2, 4, xii, xix
Alnmouth Cross   9
Alyn, Simon   139
Andrewes, Lancelot   121
Anne of Denmark, Queen   121
Anselm, Archbishop   14
Appleford, Anne   97
Arians   ix
Ashington   90
Ashley, Edwina   92, 94
Ashley, Hon. Evelyn   115, 147
Ashley, Maud   94
Ashley, Sybella   117
Ashley, Wilfred   94
Ashton   xii
Asser, Bishop   64
Athelstan, King   56
Augmentations, Court of   105
Avery, Joseph   71, 125
Avery Moore, Rev. C.   101

Bangor.   130
Barc, Jean   113, 114
Bartlett, John   142
Beaulieu   48
Becket, Thomas, Archbishop   122
Berthon, Rev. E. L.   41, 47, 82, 101, 117
Bertie, Lady Montagu   95
Bertie, Lord Montagu   94
Blowes, William   105
Boston   65

Boston, Massachusetts   126
Boulogne   122, 123
Breamore   10
Brooke, Elizabeth   55, 59, 66
Burnham, Bettrixe   139
Bury St.Edmunds   121

Calais   141
Cambridge   130
Carter, Thomas   86
Cecilia, Abbess   42
Charles I   72, 121, 143
Charles the Bold   4
Chartres   33
Chelles   4
Chester, Thomas   70
Chilworth   24
Christina   13, xiii
Clayton & Bell   117
Clerke, Simon   105
Clermont-Ferrand   xiv
Clovis, King 4, 11
Cnut, King   7, 9
Commonwealth   71
Corban, Canon William Henry Birch   118
Corpus Christi college   62, 71
Coster Organ   98
Council of Nicaea   ix
Cowper-Temple, William   85
Cranmer, Archbishop   69
Cromwell, Thomas   60
Croyland Abbey   5
Cynegils, King   2

David I, King   24
Delamere, Lady   94
Diocletian   39
Dover   xvii
Dublin   129, 130
Dunstan, Archbishop   ix
Dutton, Hon. Ralph Heneage   116

Eadred, King vii, ix
Eadwig, King 2
Eadyth 13, 14
Ealhswith xii, xix
Earl of Gloucester, Robert xiii
Earl Reginald (of Cornwall) xvii
East Winch, Norfolk xvi
Easton, Hugh 111, 117
Edgar, King 1, 2, 9, 49, 50, 59, 120, vii, viii, xii
Edgar Atheling 13
Edington 64, xii
Edmund Atheling 5, viii
Edmund Ironside, King 13
Edward I, King 120
Edward the Confessor, King 13
Edward the Elder, King 1, 2, 4, 56, 147
Edward VI, King 35, 69
Edward VII, King 94
Eggesworth, Thomas 66
Elfled 56
Elfleda 1, 4, 56
Elfrida 5
Elizabeth I, Queen 70, 120, 143
Elwina 6, 32
Emma, Queen 9
Endle, Mr. 100
Ethelfleda 4, 6, 18
Ethelred, King 7, 10
Ethelwold, Bishop 4, ix
Ethelwold, nobleman 5
Ethelwulf, King 4

Fairfax, General 72
Faithfull, Dr. 73
Fareham 130, 131, 132
Flanders, Count of 123
Flaxman, John, RA 85, 86
Fleming, Sir Francis 61, 105
Fleming, Frances 86, 90
Fleming, William 90
Florence of Worcester 1
Folyot, John 66

Fontevrault   124
Footner, Mrs. G. B.   115
Foster, John   61, 90
Fox, Bishop   39, 62
Frithestan, Bishop   56
Fuchs, Emil

Gascoigne, George   109
Gaspar   96
Gerveys, Joan   44
Giacoma de Settisoli, Lady   38
Glastonbury   121, ix
Goldering, Richard   139
Gollop, George   96
Gosport   131
Gowry conspiracy   120
Great Bedwyn   48
Greene, John   66
Guthrum   xii

Hampp, John   113
Hardgrave, Charles   116
Harvey, Agnes   53
Headbourne Worthy   10, 85
Henry I, King   13, 55, xiii
Henry II, King   122
Henry III, King   44
Henry V, King   xvi
Henry VII, King   37, 38, 90
Henry VIII, King   38, 47, 60, 120, xix
Henry de Chilmark   65
Henry, Marquess of Lansdowne   86
Hexham Abbey   34
Holiday, Henry   111, 117
Houghton   74
Huguenot   129
Hurst Castle   121

Icthe, Joan   44
Immer   64

Innocent IV, Pope   13
Isabella de Camoys   66
Isle of Wight   24

Jacob, John   142
James I, King   120, 142
Jedburgh Abbey   24
Jersey   130
Joanna   55
Judith   4
Judson, John   105

Kempe, Charles Eamer   111, 115
Kent, John   142
Kilpeck   29
King John's House   120
King, Mr. Dennis   113
King, John   55
Kingstown   129

Lady Chapel   133
Lanfranc, Archbishop   1
Langtoft, Peter de   1, 4
Latham, Dr. John   33, 34, 46, 79
Laud, William, Archbishop   70, 125
Lee Manor   95
Lillechurch   122, xvii
Liverpool   129, 130
Louis of France, King   123
Louise, Princess   147
Lymington   130, 132

Macbeth   13
Major, William   79, 85
Malcolm III, King   13
Malmesbury Abbey   97
Malmesbury, William of   2
Margaret, Queen   13
Mary de Blois   122, xiii

Mary, Queen 69
Matilda, Queen 13, 56, 122, xiii
Matthew of Alsace 123, 124
Mayo, Elizabeth 96
Mayo, William 96
Mears, Thomas 108
Merwenna 5,18
Middlemore, Mary 121
Miller, Alice 139
Minstede, John de 66
Montpellier 39
Montreuil 124
Moody, Ann 95
Morison, Professor S. E. 126
Moses, Jone 73
Mountbatten of Burma, Countess 94
Mountbatten of Burma, Earl 91, 92, 119, 120
Mount Temple, Baroness 116
Mount Temple of Lee, Lord 94, 115
Muchelney vii

Naples 130
Neill, Captain Charles 113, 115
Netley 48
Nevill, Joan de 42
New Minster 9
New Model Army 72
Nicholas de Botelston 65
Noel, Caroline 135
Noel, Hon. Gerard 82, 134
Norris, Canon Walter 97
Notre-Dame-du-Port xiv
Nunnaminster 7, xii
Nursling 3

'SS Orion' 131
Orlton, Bishop 29, 50, 62
Osborne 131, 132
Ouseley, Sir Frederick 101
Oxford Cathedral 24

Palmerston, Viscount   75, 80, 85, 95, 115, 119, 132
Park, David   32
Penmaenmawr   130
Pershore   vii, viii
Peterborough   5
Petty, Anthony   141
Petty, Sir William   86, 87, 119, 141, 143
Peverel, John   70
Pevsner   37, 43
Piers, Anne   95
Piers, William MP   95
Poitiers   xiii
Powell, James & Son   111, 115
Poyns, Margaret   55
Purkiss   14

Quarr   24

Regularis Concordia   4, ix
Richard de Lucy   xvii
Richard I, King   48
Richardson and Gill   94
Ringwood   72
Robert, Duke of Ancaster   95
Rome   130
Romesey, John de   64
Romsey, Lord   92, 120
Rowse, Joyce   59
Royal College of Surgeons   129
Rule of St. Benedict.   4, 49
Rumsey, Almaric   116
Ryprose, Elizabeth   37, 60

Sabellians   ix
Saladin   48
Salisbury   98, 120
Sandys, Lord   38
Schyrlock, William   64
Serpentine   131
Seymour, Edward   69

Seymour, Queen Jane   61
Skeat, Francis   118
Solomon de Roffe   64
Sorrento   130
Southampton   3, 65, 120
Southwell Minster   8
Spence, Charles   43, 76, 100, 134
St. Anastasia.   xix
St. Anthony   29
St. Armel   37, 38
St. Barbe family   61
St. Bathild   4
St. Benedict   37, 49, 52, 63
St. Blaise   29
St. Boniface   3
St. Catherine   29
St. Clare   38, xix
St. Clement   29
St. Cross   48
St. Cuthbert   56
St. Eadburgh   1
St. Edburga   xix
St. Edmund Hall, Oxford   125
St. Erasmus   29
St. Ethelfleda   1, 46
St. Ethelfleda's chapel   43
St. Francis   38
St. George   35
St. George, Brotherhood of   29, 34
St. George's Chapel   47, 48
St. Jerome   38
St. John   29
St. Lawrence   28
St. Lawrence's Chapel   35, 39
St. Mary's Abbey   46, 60, xix
St. Mary's Abbey, Leicester   xvii
St. Mary's Chapel   32, 44, 80, 133
St. Nicholas   7, 32, 33
St. Nicolas, Rouen   113
St. Roche   38
St. Scholastica   37
St. Sebastian   39, 38
St. Sulpice, Rennes   122

St. Swithun   38, 118
St. Swithun's Priory   62
Stanbridge Earls   96
Stephen, King   122, 124, xiii
Stork, John   142
Stratford-atte-Bow, Priory   122
Swein, King   7
Sydmonton   64

Taylor, Alice   87
Test, River   3, 6
Thacher, Anthony   125
Theobald, Archbishop   122
Third Viscount Palmerston (Prime Minister)   86
Timsbury   64
Timsbury Manor   116
'SS Titanic'   96
Tollemache, Georgina   116
Tower, Walter   115
Tozier, Clement   108
Tylee, Mrs.   100

Umfray, Joan   66
Umfray, John   26, 66

Vanderplank, John   141
Victoria, Queen   41, 92, 94, 127, 131, 137
'Victoria and Albert'   131
Virgin Mary   1

Wadham, Jane   61, 90
Wadham, Katherine   61
Wale, Richard   97
Walerand, Alice   58, 119
Walker, J. W.   101
Waller, Sir William   72, 98
Warren, John   73, 93
Warren, Thomas   73, 74, 93
Waterloo   129

Wedmore, Treaty of   xii
Wedgwood   85
Westbrooke, Anne   55, 60
Westmacott, Richard   86
Westminster Abbey   38, 86, 118
White, Anthony   71, 119
White, John   105
Whitechapel Foundry   108
Whittier, J. G.   127
William I, King   108
William II, King   13, 14
William III and Mary II   74
William of Wykeham, Bishop   26, 34, 52, 53, 59, 65, 66
Wilton Abbey   14
Winchester   3, 6, 26, 39, 48, 60, 72, 98, 118, 120, 121, xii
Windsor   131
Winfrith   3
Winthrop   127
Wolsey, Cardinal Thomas   35, 38
Wolsey, Thomas Canonicus   35
Woodburn, John   100
Woodruffe, Brian J.   108
Worcester   vii
Wyntershull, Alice de   55